HOW TO TWIRL

A lovely way to live

by

KELLY DYKSTRA

Thrill & Move
worldwide

Thrill & Move Worldwide
Otsego, Minnesota 55330

How to Twirl: A Lovely Way To Live
Copyright © 2017 by Kelly Dykstra
www.kellydykstra.com

Cover design, description & editing by Tracy Keech

ISBN-10: 0-9960223-4-1
ISBN-13: 978-0-9960223-4-7

THIS ONE'S FOR YOU

◆

Holland, Mum, Chrissie, Katie, Lily, Mom, Kristin,
Klair, Hailey, Kelli, Alanah, and all the girls I don't know
and all the girls I do.

May you lay down what weighs you and be free to live lovely lives.

CONTENTS

WHERE CREDIT IS DUE

———◆———

To a lady named Brenda, because years ago when I asked God (in private) if I should write a book (*please give me a sign!*), you baked me a cake. In the shape of a book. With the title, *How to Twirl*, in yummy pink letters.

To Grandpa and Grandma Coulter, because you indulged my twirling and flipping and trying to get the old German Shepherd to do tricks to the tune of John Philip Sousa when I put on circuses in your front yard. And because when I was waiting for God to answer me about a book, you said these words to me on the phone: "I suppose you're going to write a book next."

To Ted, because I do remember that it was you who brought the third sign. But I can't for the life of me remember what it was (see: Chapter 71).

To Tracy, because, frankly, I wouldn't want to do this without you. You analyze every word, agonize over every apostrophe, and read into every sentence. You tell me I'm funny and smart, and I'm pretty sure a good chunk of your life is spent helping me not look dumb.
I can't even.

To Eric, because you aren't satisfied with me just being your *ezer*. You make me stand up and be my own. We save each other daily, I think.

Introduction

————◆————

Last week I was talking to my friend Amy, and she told me she hates journaling. I asked why, and she said it's because she *hates* everything she writes. Like, she goes back and reads it and doesn't like what she wrote or how she came across. Being a fan of journaling as a way to get my personal issues out, I told her just don't go back and read it. But she wasn't convinced. Oh well.

I've written one sort-of book (*The Simple Journal*) and one real one (*The People Mover*), but I started this one first. I tried writing it a least four different times over the course of five years. And I *hated* everything I wrote. I hated how I came across. I tried a daily-quiet-time format with a set of scriptures to read and a bunch of room for you to journal. Or not. (Amy.) I tried organizing a plan to take you on a spiritual journey, laying a theological foundation and then layering concepts like adoption into God's family and being Spirit-controlled and fixing your mind on Jesus and recognizing the power of your words.

I sounded stiff and was literally boring *myself* when I went back and read it. Unfortunately, the don't-go-back-and-read-it philosophy that applied to Amy's journal does not apply to writing a book you hope other people will read.

As I mucked about in my old journals and blog posts, I found the kind of writing I like, and the kind other people have told me they like to read. It's just about life. Specifically, my life, since that's what's generally on my mind. And what I'm learning and what God is doing. And about marriage and parenting and cooking and traveling and leading a church and trusting God with my money and figuring crap out.

Guess what! I *don't hate* going back and reading it. In fact, every time I go back and read what I've written, I am re-inspired to stay in faith, keep trusting God, and be the best me that I can be.

So this book has absolutely no organized flow. It's just what I've written on my journey into the lovely way I've learned to live. There's no laying of foundational principles before inspiring you to deeper faith. It is not in chronological order. Some chapters will be from three years ago, and some will be from last week. Sometimes I'll give a preface for context, and sometimes I will just copy and paste it as I originally wrote it, and let it stand alone.

It's like life. A little messy, funny, meaningful, helpful, and maybe a little boring at times, but *it is what it is*.

I just hope that each day you'll find something we have in common, something that draws you to Jesus, and something to share with a friend. And I hope it inspires you to twirl.

xoxo,

Kelly

1

On Twirling

———◆———

It is a little girl's first instinct when she puts on a dress.

It is an un-self-conscious effort to show off a 360° view of herself.

If the little girl is alone, it is often done in front of a mirror.

It is best done with a full skirt that twirls so far out it's parallel to the ground.

If done repeatedly (usually in the company of other twirlers in a great big space), it results in euphoria, a delightful collapse to the ground, and unrestrained laughter.

When I was little, a woman named Rose gave me the slip that she had worn under her hoop skirt. I thought it was the most beautiful thing ever. And when I twirled, that slip spun straight out! It was the *perfect* twirly skirt. I have a vivid recollection of myself, age 7, at Aunt Ginny's house, swishing and twirling to the tune of a Strawberry Shortcake music box, in front of the sliding doors where I could see my reflection. I felt pretty and fancy, and when I twirled, I didn't care if I looked silly or got dizzy. Because I was wearing my twirly skirt, and I was beautiful and free.

Much like trying on mom's high heels and lipstick, twirling is a rite of passage for every little girl.

But it is rarely done by a grown-up.

Why? Because over time, life beats the twirl right out of you.

People trip you. You bump into things. The twirly skirt gets ripped. Your hands hold responsibilities and your shoulders carry burdens. You get a little cellulite, compelling you to keep that skirt down at all costs. You learn that the world is harsh, and you start to hang on to what little self-confidence you have. Maybe some friends ask you to dance, but you're scared they'll laugh if you try.

So you cross your arms and keep your feet flat on the ground and just wear your jeans and hide in the safe places like the kitchen or the internet or the church or the realm of motherhood.

If I twirl, I might look silly.

Or fall on my face.

If I twirl, someone might laugh.

If I twirl, the cellulite will show.

If I twirl, I might bump into someone else and make her angry with me.

If I twirl, I might lose control.

Or vomit.

Or have fun.

Maybe I'll put on the twirly skirt for a special event, and rotate slowly in front of the mirror. I'll look at myself and feel pretty. But I won't twirl, because then others will know I feel good about myself, and they might not agree. They might scorn me behind my back or smirk to my face.

"Who does she think she is, flaunting herself in public? Doesn't she know she's imperfect? She should be ashamed of all her issues... she has no right to look all twirly and stuff..."

I'll just stand very still and hold on tightly to my image and hide safely behind my defenses, my titles – mom, wife, working woman, student, entrepreneur, employee – and I will not twirl.

Because I'm grown up now, and I know better.

To twirl is not safe.

Heck, no. Twirling isn't safe. It never was.

But when you were little, you didn't care, because you had someone bigger than you looking out for you, the whole world was yours, and you felt pretty. You didn't care if your tights matched your dress or not. If you were really lucky, your mom still had some of her twirl left, and she let you wear whatever made you feel fabulous. I wore Rose's twirly slip 'til it fell apart.

I don't know when you lost your twirl. Maybe it was sudden. Maybe it was gradual. Life sneaks up sometimes. I had my first kid and cut my hair off. In my defense, I was going for Meg Ryan's look in "You've Got Mail," which did NOT work with my curly hair. I sacrificed my twirl for motherhood, because, hey, I was the ripe old age of 21. No more twirling for me!

I worked in a strict Christian school and church environment, so I did my best to conform to everyone's expectations of me. I wore the right things and tried to say the right things and tried to enjoy the right music and hung out with the right people, and basically stifled the real me. I worried (and was lectured) about what people thought and what they said about me. So I held on tightly to the things I could control and enjoy in my own little home, and I was lonely and very un-twirl-ly.

Gradually God has brought me back to a place where I can twirl. Not just a location or environment, but a place in my heart. A place where I realize that I can be confident in my unique design. God made me this way. I can be me! I can have huge responsibilities on my shoulders and still be free to twirl. I can seek to understand how God wired me and be confident in it. I don't have to worry about other people's expectations or how they feel about my choices. I can have healthy relationships and passions and joy and fun! I can have a really great first-hand look at the depths of my flaws, and still be free to twirl. I can trip and fall but still get up and keep going.

That's what I want for you, too. We'll never get it all right. We'll never feel 100% confident, but most of us can sure as heck be a lot better at it than we are right now.

For today, take a deep breath, slowly spread your arms, and turn in a circle. Imagine the twirly skirt ruffling out. Imagine giving a full 360° view of yourself to God and knowing He approves.

He approves. He nods and smiles and winks and says, "That's my girl. I made her *just like that!*"

And that's the only voice that matters.

Close your eyes and breathe in His approval. Forget everything else except the little girl in you and the Great Big Creator watching out for you. You can twirl again. You can move through life with open arms, a generous heart, and the confidence to change your world.

2

To Twirl, Spot

———◆———

My daughter Holland started taking dance lessons at age 4. I'll never forget her first recital... seeing her little pudgy legs under the red and white polka-dot costume, tapping away to "Elmo You Can Drive My Car." I was so proud, especially when she picked her bloomer wedgie out of her bootie.

Once she was finished, I was able to sit back and enjoy watching the more advanced dancers. The show was phenomenal, and I'll tell you one of the things that fascinated me most: how those dancers can twirl and twirl and twirl in one place, without careening around and banging into other people. If I tried to do that, I'd be like a top I used to play with as a kid—I would twirl my way across the stage and right off the edge.

I found out that when a dancer does turns like that, she picks a spot on a wall or across the room at eye level, that she focuses on every time her head rotates. It's called "spotting". She focuses on that spot as long as she can, then whips her head around, and returns to the spot again. The spot doesn't move; she does. Everything else around her flies by as she turns, but the spot she has chosen to look to for stability is constant. As long as she "spots", she can turn safely and keep balance and perspective even though she's twirling. If she loses the spot, she loses perspective. It is her guide.

To twirl successfully through life, we must spot. We have to chose one thing we seek out and look to as the constant, unchanging guide that we fix our eyes on. Everything around us becomes a blur as it moves and changes, but we can always spot the source of our balance and perspective. Our twirl begins and ends with a focus on the "spot".

God says, *I am the same yesterday, today, and forever! Hebrews 13:8*

So, *Let us fix our eyes on Jesus, the author and perfecter of our faith...* *Hebrews 12:2*

Author and perfecter.

Author = The One who picked up the pen and started writing your faith story.

Perfecter = The One who will work out that faith story perfectly.

Spotters = Me. You. The ones who keep our eyes on the unchanging One so we never twirl ourselves right off the edge.

3

Mornings

———————◆———————

You know, once a twirling top gets bumped and starts to wobble, it rarely recovers and begins spinning in balance again, right? It's like that for our daily twirl, too. Choose to find your spot when you wake up in the morning, before you pick up your phone or jump in the shower or start twirling your day away with your focus on whatever comes up that you have to deal with.

The Psalms speak often about spotting God in the morning.

Listen to my voice in the morning, LORD. Each morning I bring my requests to you and wait expectantly. Psalm 5:3

Satisfy us each morning with your unfailing love, so we may sing for joy to the end of our lives. Psalm 90:14

Let me hear of your unfailing love each morning, for I am trusting you. Show me where to walk, for I give myself to you. Psalm 143:8

Now, I'll be honest with you. I don't like mornings. I resonate a little more with this verse:

A loud and cheerful greeting early in the morning will be taken as a curse! Proverbs 27:14

In other words, if you're a happy morning person, *back off* until I've had my coffee and time with God.

But anyway, it is SO worth investing the morning time to get centered and find your spot before you start twirling.

Here are a few tips that might help.

- *Knees before feet.* Before your feet hit the floor in the morning, hit your knees (figuratively or literally) in prayer. Ask God to help you be sensitive to His leading and to guide and bless your day.

- *Develop a coffee habit.* OK, that's not what I really mean, but the thing that keeps me spotting God each morning is the fact that I sit on the couch and drink coffee with Him. I require coffee almost as much as I require God's power in my life, so I fill up with both at the same time. Arrange what you need to look forward to your time with God. A comfy chair, candle, snuggly throw, tea, coffee, quiet music, whatever. (Unless it puts you back to sleep.)

- *Read a Bible that you can understand.* There are many versions of the Bible. There are some that read like Shakespeare, some written on a sixth-grade level, and everything in between. Presently, I use the New Living Translation. I enjoy it because it's different from what I memorized as a child, so it helps me "hear" Scripture in a new, fresh way.

- *Use a devotional book (like this one!) or reading guide to give you a place to start.* That's somewhat more purposeful than randomly opening your Bible and closing your eyes and pointing to a verse for the day.

- *Ask God two questions:*

    - *God, show me You.* (Show me Your truth in Scripture.

Show me what You're like so I can learn to trust You more and share Your love with others. Show me the benefits that are mine because I'm your girl.)

- *God, show me, me.* (Show me what You are changing in my life. Show me where I've done wrong and need to ask forgiveness from others or offer forgiveness to others. Show me what I need to let You work on so I can twirl through life more gracefully.)

- *Write something.* You don't have to journal, Amy. At the very least, circle the most interesting Scripture you read in your Bible. If you can manage more than that, copy the Bible verse onto paper. And maybe write out a prayer for your day. The act of expressing words in written form helps to solidify thoughts and truth and helps you remember it. I'm not saying you have to become a journaling freak. Just put down some evidence that you spent time with God that morning.

- *Pray.* God is a good Father who wants to walk through your day with you. Start a conversation that continues throughout the day.

4

Jeez, Take a Compliment

———◆———

I've been reading the story of Mary, the mother of Jesus. She's pretty famous. She's a saint; practically an angel. No one ever says anything negative about her.

Except me.

You ever notice Mary can't take a compliment? Yeah, I went there. I said something negative about Mary Motherofjesus.

> *God sent the angel Gabriel to Nazareth, a village in Galilee, to a virgin named Mary. She was engaged to be married to a man named Joseph, a descendant of King David. Gabriel appeared to her and said, "Greetings, favored woman! The Lord is with you!" Confused and disturbed, Mary tried to think what the angel could mean. Luke 1:26-29*

An angel FROM HEAVEN gave the girl a compliment, and she was *confused* and *disturbed* by it.

Gabriel: "Hey, Mary! You're favored by God, and He's with you!"

Mary: "Me? What? I—I mean, what?"

Isn't it crazy how hard it is for a woman to take a compliment? I mean, tell a guy he looks good, and he'll puff out his chest and be all like, "I know, right?"

But you? Does this ever happen?

Someone compliments your outfit, and you proceed to tell them why it isn't so special.

Oh, this old thing?

I got this at the thrift store.

Yeah, but it has a stain on it right here.

Someone compliments your hair, and you explain why it looks that way.

Haha! It's funny you say that, because it's like three days dirty!

Yeah, but check out the gray...

Oh my gosh, the humidity is making it crazy!

Someone compliments your ability, and you pooh-pooh their opinion.

I just fake it.

My team makes me look good.

Oh, jeez. Anyone could do it.

Someone compliments your personality/character, and you just turn it around on them.

Wow! I always think the same thing about you!

Oh, I know you're such a better woman than me...

Aren't you so sweet! You always say the nicest things!

Your husband comments about how hot you are, and you discredit him.

You have to say that. You're married to me.

Good thing love is blind.

Whatever.

If you can't take a compliment or statement of blessing over you, especially from your own husband or close friend, you may need to re-think your life a bit.

Once I told April, a woman in my church, "Your lipstick always looks so good!" Her reply was matter-of-fact. "I know. I have really great lips."

My friend Tara was wearing a cute hat one day, and I told her so. She replied, "Thanks! I don't usually wear hats because my hair is too good, but..."

Both of these conversations happened years ago, but they've stuck with me because it's so unusual for a woman to receive a compliment so casually and then to speak so confidently about her asset.

Did you know that God gave you your unique look, talent, taste, and abilities, and He moves others to notice and compliment you? God speaks through the people around you! When you negate their compliment, you cheat them out of the blessing of obeying God. When you just turn the compliment around on them, you steal some of the joy they get from being an encouragement. Plus, it's like He's giving you a gift through them, and you're throwing it back in His face! Who would do that to God?

Be OK with receiving positive words from people (and God).

Go look yourself in the mirror and practice.

"Hello, you look lovely today!"

"Why, thank you!"

Look how easy that was!

5

The Antidote to Fear

———◆———

Gabriel appeared to her and said, "Greetings, favored woman! The Lord is with you!" Confused and disturbed, Mary tried to think what the angel could mean. "Don't be afraid, Mary," the angel told her, "for you have found favor with God!" Luke 1:28-30

The angel shows up and greets Mary. He guesses (correctly) that she was freaking out a little bit, so he tries to ease her fear right off the bat (because who can focus on *anything* when you're scared out of your freaking mind?). Before we discuss his solution, let's talk about fear.

What are you afraid of?

There are dumb things like spiders and clowns, and then there are the devastating things like cancer and bankruptcy.

But I'm talking about the middle-weight fears. The ones that motivate you to behave certain ways over the course of a day.

We don't like to admit fear, but think about it: feelings of frustration or anger or acting in a way that is, shall we say, *less than our potential*, can usually be traced back to a root fear that is driving our outward behavior.

Maybe these sound familiar:

You get angry at your kids because they don't do their chores.

Fear of not being a good mom.

You get frustrated with your husband/roommate when he/she doesn't help around the house.

Fear of being stuck with all the work.

You shoot a terse email to a coworker after they corrected you in a meeting.

Fear of people thinking you're not smart or capable.

You freak out about an unexpected bill.

Fear of not having enough.

You continue to date someone who clearly does not share your values.

Fear of being alone.

Some fears are valid. It DOES suck to not have enough money or be stuck carrying the workload in your home. But when fear plants the seeds, the fruit is sour. Lashing out damages relationships. Then you feel bad about yourself, so then you have the fear, the issue, the damaged relationship, *and* the guilt.

What's the antidote to fear? Courage? Faith?

Nah. The angel's response to Mary's fear was NOT, "Hey, lady. Have faith! Put on your big girl panties and get tough."

He said "Don't be afraid, for you have found favor with God!"

The reason she shouldn't be afraid was because when the God of the universe looked at her, He felt His heart swell with love and favor. And she had not even done anything special yet!

The antidote to fear is not faith. It is knowing you are loved.

More specifically, it's the perfect, un-failing, un-mistake-making, un-forgetful, un-demanding, un-earned kind of love that comes from God your Father simply because He's your Dad and you're His girl.

We know how much God loves us, and we have put our trust in his love... Such love has no fear, because perfect love expels all fear. 1 John 4:16a-18a

I don't know what fears are simmering below the surface of your soul, but today why don't you try this:

- Pay attention to those moments when you react poorly
- Identify the fear that might be driving that reaction
- Take a deep breath and say aloud, *I am loved, favored, cared for, and I'll be just fine,* and then...
- Modify your reaction from a place of being fully loved.

In other words, return to your "spot" as you twirl. It's going to be OK.

6

But How?

———◆———

OK, this is the last one on Mary.

> *"Don't be afraid, Mary," the angel told her, "for you have found favor with God! You will conceive and give birth to a son, and you will name him Jesus. He will be very great and will be called the Son of the Most High. The Lord God will give him the throne of his ancestor David. And he will reign over Israel forever; his Kingdom will never end!" Mary asked the angel, "But how can this happen? I am a virgin." Luke 1:30-34*

Have you ever tried to tell someone good news who, instead of reacting with the enthusiasm you were hoping for, totally popped your balloon by asking, "But how?"

"Guess what! I got a new car!"

> *"But how many miles does it have?"*

"Good news! We signed that lease!"

> *"But how many years? It better be at least two."*

"Hey honey! We're going on vacation!"

"But how will we pay for that?"

GAAAAAH.

I imagine that's how the angel felt when he delivered this great news to Mary about how God picked HER to get to do something awesome, and she was just like, "But how?!"

GAAAAAH.

Let's try to eliminate practical-brain for a second and imagine that God is looking at you and saying, "I like you SO much that I have mapped out a whole life story for you and I want to walk it out with you!"

Wait a minute. You don't have to imagine that. You can just read where He actually *wrote* it in the Bible for you to read. The Psalmist (David) wrote what he knew to be truth about how God lovingly creates us with purpose.

> *You go before me and follow me. You place your hand of blessing on my head...You saw me before I was born. Every day of my life was recorded in your book. Every moment was laid out before a single day had passed. Psalm 139:5, 16*

When you hear that, does your mind immediately leap to questioning? But how *is God's hand of blessing on my head? Does He really know everything? If He did, wouldn't he reject me?*

When you hear a really cool truth from Scripture or God whispers a dream into your heart, or someone identifies and calls out your potential, do you say, "that sounds awesome," or do you start asking questions and qualifiers and try to wrap your brain around it?

But how could that be true?

But how would that ever happen?

But how… but how… but how…

Here's your challenge for today: when you read a promise or truth in Scripture or when someone tells you something good, don't start with, "But how?" Don't start looking for ways to make it make sense or explain it or figure it out.

Just be *in the moment* and take the gift as it is given.

I know sometimes these things blind-side you. Just pause. Take a deep breath, and say, "OK, God, you've got this!"

It turned out pretty well for Mary, so you'll probably be fine, too.

7

Birds and Biscuits

———————◆———————

I killed a bird.

It wasn't a crow or a goose or some other I-could-potentially-hit-it-with-my-car-and-not-feel-bad fowl type.

It was one of those sweet, little, innocent, fluttery birds.

You know, the kind about which the term "bird brain" was coined. The kind that bonk into our windows at home and then lie there, stunned, on our deck, until we get bored of watching and praying and scare them into an off-kilter flight to recuperate somewhere else.

THUNK. Right off the hood of my minivan and then onto the road.

Note: I am not an animal-lover. Animals are nice enough. They serve a purpose. I was passionate about horses when I was younger and cried when we had to put down Candy, my Palomino. But I don't understand why my friends are devastated when their animals die. I hug them and look sympathetic, and have even sent flowers. But I don't really understand that kind of grief about... well... an *animal.*

So when this little bird-brain became dead because of me (though totally beyond my control), I was surprised to feel a lump in my throat and tears welling up.

It must have been the *imago Dei*. One of the times the image of God stamped on my soul comes out, despite me.

Baffled by my emotion, I started considering, "Do I really care that much about that bird?" Uh, not really. What was really getting me was these verses, which popped into my head (thanks, Mrs. Grantham, 6th grade Sunday School Teacher at Ewell Bible Baptist Church).

What is the price of two sparrows—one copper coin? But not a single sparrow can fall to the ground without your Father knowing it. And the very hairs on your head are all numbered. So don't be afraid; you are more valuable to God than a whole flock of sparrows. Matthew 10:29-31

If I feel this way about a bird I *didn't even know*, how must my Father feel about me? Me, whose hairs He keeps counted. (And I have a LOT of hairs. Which fall out at an alarming rate. Ask my husband, who finds them plastered in large clumps to the shower wall.)

My Father knows I stubbed my toe Sunday night. Hard. You shoulda heard it crack.

He knows I killed one of His creatures on Monday morning.

He knows I ate roast beef Monday night, forgetting how ill it makes me. He was there as I lay in bed cursing that roast beef in the wee hours of Tuesday morning.

He knows I second-guessed decisions I made on Wednesday.

He knows I felt mom-guilt for feeding my family fried food and empty carbs at dinner out last night, because I'm a working mother who can't always get the nutritious-meal thing down.

He was with me between 2 and 4 this morning as I prayed for

members of our staff family who are hurting; thanking God for the ground-breaking celebration last night for our building project, and begging Him to take care of it all.

To take care of *us* all.

And He was like, *"Pssht. I cared about the bird. I think I've got y'all covered."* (In my mind this morning, God's from the South.)

I am deeply loved. Highly favored.

You know how I know?

My assistant, Whitney, brought me a biscuit & gravy from Hardee's. My absolute favorite breakfast food, which I haven't had in probably a year and a half. She said, and I quote, "God told me to get my butt out of bed and drive to Hardee's."

He's a really good Father. If He cares about the bird, if He told Whitney to get me a biscuit, I'm thinking He can also handle the big stuff just fine.

My stuff. Your stuff. We're His kids.

Deeply loved. Highly favored.

8

Guilty Pleasures

---◆---

Lately I've been de-stressing by way of Words With Friends. It started last fall when I had back surgery, and I spent many recovery hours playing this game that I love. I grew up playing Scrabble with my mom—it's still a favorite when my mom and sisters and I get together. Words is nice because I can play with friends (I'm BEATING you, Jason) and strangers, too. It satisfies my appetite for competition. Plus, I've heard that word games will stave off dementia in my old age. It's almost as important as eating vegetables.

I also enjoy Candy Crush, and I'm presently on level 1,032. I often play it on flights when I can't connect to the internet. While Words is a smart-people game, Candy Crush… well… I feel a little bit embarrassed that someone with a college degree, hopes and dreams for the future, and a clearly broadcast mission in life would be wasting time on such a ridiculous game.

What if people think I'm a lazy time-wasting game-playing couch potato?

So I feel a little guilty.

Recently I heard someone use the term "guilty pleasure" to refer to a show she watches. And I immediately had a red flag pop up in my mind.

Guilty pleasure.

People, we should not have guilty pleasures.

If it makes you feel guilty, it should not be a pleasure.

Either get rid of the guilt, or get rid of the pleasure.

Guilty pleasure makes sin sound tasty. Like three pieces of chocolate cake or a flirty conversation with someone else's husband.

Either the guilt is for good reason or it is not.

What is your guilty pleasure? Horror movies? Graphic romance novels? Reality TV? Chocolate? Coffee? Online relationships? Hours lost to YouTube? A simple game like Candy Crush that grabs you and keeps you from accomplishing anything meaningful?

Ask yourself some questions:

"Does it make me feel guilty because I know it doesn't please God?"

"Does it make me feel guilty because I enjoy it in excess?"

"Does it make me feel guilty because I'm afraid someone else will judge me, so I impose the guilt on myself?"

"Should it even make me feel guilty at all?"

Hold the pleasure up to God and look at it through His eyes.

It might be that your guilty pleasure shouldn't actually make you feel guilty. That it's false guilt that cheats you from enjoying a gift God has given you to enjoy.

It might be that your guilty pleasure is sin – something that is not rooted in faith and does not line up with God's best for your life – and you need to eradicate it from your life.

Either enjoy your pleasure as a gift from God within the bounds of His blessing, or stop sinning.

Now I'm off to play Candy Crush, because it's my day off, and I've already taken my Words turns.

9

Moods and Rings

———◆———

This week I was given a mood ring. It's kind of fascinating to see how the colors change as I go through my day. My Facebook status yesterday mentioning the color of my mood ring sparked plenty of comments and links to color charts so I could gauge my mood.

It's funny, really, that I was trying to figure out my mood based on the color of the ring, rather than vice versa.

Interesting how so often we aren't really aware of our mood, or, more importantly, the state of our hearts.

Which brings me to the mood ring of sorts that God has provided to gauge the state of our hearts: His Spirit. Scripture says when we choose Jesus as our Leader, His Spirit comes to hang out in our hearts. This is pretty great because He comforts us, brings peace, convicts us of our sin, guides us into truth and reminds of us what we have learned so that we can live it out.

> *But the Helper (Comforter, Advocate, Intercessor—Counselor, Strengthener, Standby), the Holy Spirit, whom the Father will send in My name [in My place, to represent*

Me and act on My behalf], He will teach you all things.
And He will help you remember everything that I have told
you. John 14:26 (AMP)

The fruit (results) of the Spirit of God living in us is love, joy, peace, goodness, meekness, faith, self-control... (Galatians 5:22-23) but we have to live tuned-in to that Spirit. The world and situations will always shout louder than Him. But, WHAT POWER we have when we live according to His guidance.

Oh, how we can stay on track when we let Him gauge our moods and guide us into positive change and wise living.

If only He were just a little more tangible. Or visible. So we wouldn't forget. Like a mood ring.

Hmmm... here's a thought. My mood ring will remind me to stop and listen to the Spirit's counsel as to the state of my heart. Suddenly it's not so silly anymore.

Draw a little smiley face on your hand today, and when you notice it, check for a second to see if the state of your mood matches up with the Holy Spirit's fruit. Do you feel peaceful or anxious? Confused or clear? Exhausted or rested? Worried or grateful? Out-of-control or composed? Take that moment to ask God's Spirit to give you what you need to return to a place of faith *inside* and see how it impacts your *outside*.

10

The Caretaker's Granddaughter

———◆———

Part 1: The Estate

For the first 20 years of my life, my Grandpa and Grandma Coulter were the caretakers of a gorgeous, 100-acre estate on Lake Michigan in Wisconsin. It was built in the 1920's by Joseph Uihlein (pronounced *E* line) as his family's summer home. You don't recognize his name, but if Schlitz beer rings a bell, that's the family. (It's Wisconsin, people. They do two things there: beer and cheese.) The Uihlein family is connected by marriage to the Pabst family. Maybe you recognize that name. If you do, you get a blue ribbon.

The sign by the road said Afterglow Farm. We called it Grandpa's farm. Stone columns topped by sculptures of pineapples framed the gate that opened to a long, winding gravel driveway. (Shortly after getting my driver's license, I slid Grandpa's new midnight-blue Ford truck right into one of those columns. But that's another story. In my defense, I was an Alabama girl driving on snow and ice for the first time. It was also the second time in my life I heard my Grandpa say a bad word. It started with "s". I was scared to death.)

My grandparents lived in the remodeled upper floor of the horse barn where polo ponies were originally kept. Living in a barn sounds not-so-cool, but it was absolutely wonderful to me. It was "our" slice of the estate. The picture window in Grandpa and Grandma's bedroom revealed a pond with two islands: one accessible by a questionable wooden bridge, the other only reachable in winter, after Grandpa tested the ice for us. (If it would hold Grandpa's generous weight, it would certainly hold us kids.)

The dining table sat in front of another giant picture window, where we would eat Grandma's homemade raspberry-currant jelly on bakery bread (Grandpa never bought regular bread; he said it had "too much air in it") and watch the antics of the birds and squirrels around the bird feeders. On rare occasions, we'd see a fox looking for the kitchen scraps Grandma always left in a little pile on the sloped front lawn.

My best birthday memories were at Grandpa's farm. We had hot dogs and brats (a.k.a. bratwurst – it's a northern thing) and pork 'n' beans, which we'd scoop up with potato chips. And dill pickles. Grandma ALWAYS had homemade dill pickles. The "baby" ones were the best. We'd have a hayride with my cousins and sometimes friends I'd made at Grandpa's church on our many visits.

The estate was once a functioning farm, but not the kind you might picture up there in Dairyland. There was a horse barn, but also a peacock house. It was a fancy farm. Ornate. Flag poles and dog kennels and pump houses and goose and turkey houses – everything was framed by rocks, and chunks of colored stones and crystals were worked into everything from sculptures to doorframes to sundial stands. Metal signs hung from wrought iron identified the animal for which each building was created. I loved the horse weathervane on top of the barn.

Phrases in German were hung here and there. Headstones under a small grove of trees memorialized family members. Another few trees near a pond shaded miniature gravestones for family dogs gone before. Grass paths wound past ponds, through woods, ravines, a birch grove, a pine grove, and around a field to the top of the bluff where my cousins and I would leave our bikes and hike down the steep path along a wooded ravine to a stretch of privately-owned beach on Lake Michigan. We rarely saw another soul as we braved the chilly waters and threw dead fish at each other.

The Estate House was a mansion, in my childhood mind. Well, I suppose it's still a mansion to me now, now that I think about it. A vast home filled with antiques and big feather beds that were so high, stools were provided. The lamps in the living room dripped with crystals that shot rainbows across the room on sunny days. A pink chaise lounge in one bedroom always beckoned to me when I'd get to go inside with Grandpa so he could "check the house" and wind the big grandfather clock in the coatroom where a raccoon once came in through the chimney.

I also took great delight in finding and pressing the little button hidden under the head of the dining table. It buzzed in the kitchen. Imagine being so rich that you simply pressed a button to call your butler to serve you! The house had servant's quarters above the kitchen, accessible by a very tiny, very steep set of stairs. Stone patios with roll-out awnings provided a view of the pond in front or the garden in back. Beauty was everywhere, even in winter, when snow capped all the sculptures.

The huge garden was shaped like a wagon wheel, and in the center was a fountain that served as my personal swimming pool as a child. In my mind's eye, I will always see my grandma working in the garden, in the shadow of that huge estate house. That's where I developed a love for big pink peonies. And a fascination with garter snakes. Grandma did not love those.

I'm told that Joseph's wife Ilma Uihlein (my family has always referred to her as "Grandma Uihlein," as if we were part of their family), in her final years, enjoyed holding me while her nurse wheeled us through the garden to enjoy the fruit of *my* Grandma's labors. I don't remember this, as I was an infant, but they say she adored little Kelly. (I mean, really, who wouldn't?)

As I grew up, the Uihlein family rarely used the house. Every now and then, Grandpa would get a call that a family member was coming for a day or two. Grandma would dust and change the bed sheets, put some flowers in a vase; Grandpa would make sure there was wood for the fireplaces, and he'd leave the gate open. Mostly, though, the house just sat there empty. What a waste of such a fabulous place.

I spent many childhood hours dreaming that I lived in that big house. When I was a teenager, I recall asking Grandpa if my friend Tammy and I could spend the night over "at the Estate". The answer was no, of course. It wasn't for us. We weren't part of the family. We weren't of that class. Grandpa didn't live in the estate house. We lived over at the barn. Which was cool.

But still.

To pretend for one night that I belonged there. That I was wealthy. And classy. Entitled to be there... how amazing would that be?

After all, I already had the run of the place. The gardens and fields and paths and berry patches and barns and buildings and ponds and private beach. It felt like mine! The summer I graduated from high school, I had a boy-girl overnight party at the farm – the guys camped on the beach, and the girls and I took over Grandma's living room. I felt like I owned the place.

Except: I wasn't the rich kid.

I was the caretaker's granddaughter.

Even now, when I go back to see the farm, I feel a small sense of entitlement that is completely unjustified. "I'm Bill Coulter's granddaughter," does not carry the weight that, "I'm Joe Uihlein's granddaughter" would.

I still feel just a little bit of longing, like it's a home—a life—I could have had.

11

The Caretaker's Granddaughter

———◆———

Part 2: A Life Longed For

Do you ever feel like you were made for a better life than the one you have?

Do you ever finish a book or walk out of a movie thinking, *that's how my life should have been*?

There's a reason we long for the castle. The fluffy feather beds. The flowers. The servants and the sparkly things.

It's in our blood. We are daughters of the Estate of Heaven, and our family does not live in the barn. We are drawn to beauty because it's what we were born for.

We are drawn to bubble baths, fuzzy slippers, a crackling fireplace, pretty shoes, shiny cars, sparkly stones, delicious food... because they represent the entitled life, the class for which we were created.

We're unique, each of us, so the Estate may look different in your dreams than mine.

Either way, it's OK to dream of more. To close your eyes and imagine what life could be like IF...

Now, if you're even remotely like me, when you get a glimpse of *that life*, you close your eyes, take a deep breath, and think, *What can I do to get a life like that? Or at least a better life than the one I'm in?*

You start making a list of how you could manage your money better or keep your house cleaner or wear more stylish clothes or indulge in pleasure... you try to figure out how you can work out your own version of the Estate. I usually do this after a vacation. I want to come home and live... better. Happier. Classier.

But can we really work our way up from caretaker's granddaughter to little rich girl? Financially, I suppose. But are we able to change our own identity, the true essence of who we are, by hard work?

Consider this.

The Uihlien Estate. I belonged there. My grandparents lived there more than anyone else. I even worked for a place there! I spent days mowing those paths and lawns. I scraped paint and hauled watering cans, sprayed ferns and weeded the asparagus bed in my polka-dotted swimsuit until my back was sunburnt. I deadheaded lilies and dragged brush and watched it burn and chipped the weeds out of the pebbly garden walkways. I washed windows and picked berries and planted flowers and helped pull cattails out of the pond.

If any kid deserved a place at the Uihlein Estate, it was me. My grandparents worked for it. I worked for it. We earned it, right?

Well, actually, what we, the Coulter family *earned*, was the gratitude and benevolence of the Uihlein/Pabst family. To this day, my Grandpa and Grandma receive Christmas gifts from members of the family. We can drive onto the property, ask permission to look around, and see what the new caretakers have done to the place.

But we have to ask permission. We're not in the family.

The problem is, a place in the family is not earned by any amount of investment or work.

A place in the family is inherited by birth.

It's in the blood.

Oh, if only I had that blood.

***

There is an Estate far grander than what Joseph Uihlein built for his family.

There is wealth beyond anything a brewing empire could amass.

There is a family whose blood runs thick with entitlement.

A position in this family cannot be earned through hard work or investment.

It can only be inherited by blood.

And I have – I HAVE – that blood!

I have been born into the family of the King of the Universe.

That's me. It is the true essence of who I am.

I was separated from the family by the choices of my original parents. The consequences? I had to work hard for a place in this world. I was destined to struggle and worry and make my own way.

But Jesus.

Oh, the sweetest words ever.

But Jesus paid the price for me to be adopted back into the family, and I got to regain my rightful place as a daughter of the Estate. With all the privileges and benefits and responsibilities that come with living in a privileged family. And this is nothing I could work for. No amount of effort does this for me. HE does this for me.

Happy sigh.

So it turns out I'm in that family, after all.

But... are you?

***

What if you and I are sisters? What if we have the same blood? We were both created to be in the family of God, our Dad, the King. But because of dark forces, the sin and shame that keep humanity from our holy God, we were separated. If what the Bible says is true, this is quite alarming to me: this idea that I have sisters who are still missing from my family.

Please come home.

We may have never met. We may never meet until Heaven one day. But *I want you to regain your place in the family, like I have.*

It's your own choice, and now that you've read this, you pretty much have no excuse for staying in the barn. Scripture tells us that it's brilliantly simple, really.

If you confess with your mouth that Jesus is Lord and believe in your heart that God raised him from the dead, you will be saved. Romans 10:9

If you'd like to take this first step into the life for which you were created, I invite you to pray out loud, something like this:

"Jesus, I have gone my own way, done my own thing, and I have found that it's a life of struggle, worry, and disappointment. I want to choose a better way. Thank You for giving Your life to give me life. I receive the forgiveness You offer, I make You the Leader of my life, and I want to live in Your family, allowing You to take me through each day with joy and confidence that comes from knowing I'm a daughter of the King."

If you prayed that with sincerity of your soul, I believe that you just received your key to the Estate. You took your first step into a new life of blessing and happy abundance that comes with being in the family.

Welcome home.

HOW TO TWIRL

12

A Tale of Two Bottles

◆

No one will ever eat the rest of brownies that are in my kitchen. When I return there in a few minutes to make lunch, I'll be scraping the entire rest of the pan into the trash can.

If you share my passion for all things fudgy, you may be feeling a lump in your throat as you imagine such a precious work of culinary genius sliding sadly down into the coffee filters, used Clorox wipes, and empty hot dog packaging. But your sorrow would be misguided.

Here's why: Those brownies were made with the wrong oil.

Here's how it went down: Every now and then, Holland delights our entire family by whipping up a batch of cookies or brownies. A few nights ago, she did just that. The house smelled yummy, and the minute that pan came out of the oven, she pulled one out, poured a glass of milk, and came into the living room.

Me: "They're done?"

Her: "Yes, but they taste awful. I messed them up somehow."

Me *(you're crazy—there's no way to mess up a brownie mix)*: "What's

47

the matter with them?"

Her *(wearily)*: "I have no idea."

I didn't believe her, so I went and cut myself a chunk and popped it into my mouth. Immediately I knew the problem. I walked over to the pantry and looked at the shelf. Yep. Side-by-side were two bottles. I sighed. It was my fault.

Me: "Holland, you used the already-opened bottle of oil, right?"

Her: "Yeah."

Me: "I'm so sorry, honey. I didn't tell you. That's my used fry oil."

***

I used to have a Fry Daddy, which is like a Crock Pot, only for deep-frying things. I simply stored my oil in it and plugged it in when needed. I'd strain it when done and store it for next time. Occasionally I'd change the oil with a fresh bottle. A while back, I threw away the Fry Daddy. Now I fry on my stovetop and strain, store, and re-use the oil a few times before disposing it.

I forgot to tell Holland about it. So she used 1/3 cup of used fry oil in brownies, and they tasted fuuuuuuunky.

When I use that oil later this week to make some fries, wontons, or fish, it will taste deliiiiiiicious.

What's the difference? That oil, while it started out just like the other bottle, has been seasoned in a way that doesn't go with the flavor of brownies. It has had some life experience and earned some flavor that makes it perfect... for a different recipe. When Holland mistakenly used it for a purpose the OTHER oil was suited for, the brownies were edible, but not quite right.

What's my point? Well, I was thinking. We all start out like clean oil.

Fresh and new, ready to be used for whatever our Creator/Chef dreams up. We learn and grow and gain experience and seasoning. Based on our life's experiences and education and seasons, we become suited for certain things and not-so-suited for others. We get some things so very right and other things so very wrong, and this is all a part of our unique seasoning.

I think the goal is to just be a full bottle of who we're created to be, and let God decide how to use us. He's fully informed on where we'll bring the best flavor. He won't say, "Oops. I used the wrong oil. Why didn't somebody tell me what was in there?!" He knows what's in there already, and He will make sure we blend perfectly into just the right recipes at the right times to make something that people get to experience with delight.

And they will compliment the Chef.

You might feel like used fry oil that got poured into brownies.

You might feel like that fresh bottle left on the shelf while someone else is getting used.

Or maybe you're happily bubbling in your perfect pot while friends dance around you like French fries.

Wherever you are in this part of your seasoning, trust the Chef. Don't look around and compare. Don't wish your season away. Don't jump out of whatever recipe He has put you in. And don't try to jump into a recipe you're not meant for.

Trust His process, and trust that He's creating something delicious with your life.

For we are God's masterpiece. He has created us anew in Christ Jesus, so we can do the good things he planned for us long ago.
Ephesians 2:10

13

The Day God Made Sure I Had Cool Shoes

———◆———

Don't you tell me God doesn't care about the little things that you care about.

It's Saturday night. I'm standing on The Crossing stage before church, discussing a service-order change with Pastor Ted, and I'm wearing a great pair of black high heels.

I. Really. Love. These. Shoes. Jessica Simpson brand. Sturdy heel. Hidden platform. Got 'em at Plato's Closet for cheap. They're a staple of my wardrobe.

As I talk with Ted, I feel my foot doing something funny. I look down, and the heel of my right shoe has simply given up. It folded like the lawn chair I was sitting in at the Wild West Days parade while very pregnant with Aidan. (Shut up.)

Shoot. I live a half hour away, and the service starts in like eight minutes.

Flash back to Thursday. Whitney texts me a picture of a pair of black suede heels sitting on my desk.

I text back, "Oooooooooohhhh!"

She says, "A woman brought you these. They're in your office."

Flash forward to Saturday night. I calmly throw my shoes in the trash (sniff, sniff), and barefoot it up to my office, where I slide on the perfect pair of shoes for my outfit. I go right back to work with no loss of fashion. (My other option, had God NOT foreseen my problem and pre-provided, were nasty brown flip-flops I brought along to wear to the baptism at the lake later that evening.)

He PRE-PROVIDED. It was done. Three days before I even knew I had a problem, God had planted into the heart of a sweet woman named Donna, to bring me some shoes she knew I'd love. I hadn't even looked at them yet when my Saturday shoes broke. But I knew the answer was upstairs, waiting for me. And I went and claimed it.

Listen. This is a lesson we all need to learn.

When you have a need, as God's kid, He has PRE-PROVIDED for it.

It's done. Your job is to KNOW the answer is "upstairs" and stay calm until you get to claim it.

And don't you think, "Well, shoes are easy. A mortgage payment is way harder."

For GOD?!!! Ha. Your logic is lacking.

The earth is the Lord's and everything in it. Psalm 24:1

God has already moved in the heart of somebody, somewhere, somehow, to meet your need. He is not surprised that your dishwasher just broke, or your roof leaks, or your medical bills just came.

The answer is "upstairs". He has pre-provided the answer to your problem. Stay calm. Trust Him until you get to claim His provision.

I really love my new shoes. I really really love that my God knows about my shoe thing, and blessed me by speaking my language.

14

Face or Hands?

———◆———

On vacation in Colorado this summer, I had the unique opportunity to attend a church service in the hotel where we were staying. Being a church planter, I'm accustomed to churches being held in a variety of places; heck, The Crossing has met in a movie theater, school gym, school lunchroom, Methodist church, and a bar. So church in a hotel meeting room really wasn't a stretch for me. In fact, I felt a certain respect for the greeter standing in the hall with his stack of bulletins, smiling at all the vacationers walking by on their way to the breakfast room or the pool. So I went to my room, threw on some jeans, and went to church.

I don't remember much about what the pastor said that morning, but the one thing that stuck actually made its way to the top line of my prayer list.

Seek His face; not just His hands.

I've prayed that each day (OK, each day I've prayed through my list) since that vacation. Seek HIM, not just what He can DO for me.

Usually we pray for things.

For God to do things.

For Him to provide things.

For Him to change things.

We pray for the works of His hands.

But He wants us to seek His face.

Look to the LORD and his strength; seek his face always. 1 Chronicles 16:11

If my people, who are called by my name, will humble themselves and pray and seek my face and turn from their wicked ways, then I will hear from heaven, and I will forgive their sin and will heal their land. 2 Chronicles 7:14

My heart says of you, "Seek his face!" Your face, LORD, I will seek. Psalm 27:8

So I've been praying this each day, before I go through all my requests for Him to DO stuff in my life.

God, let me seek Your face and not just Your hands.

What does that mean? I guess it's a general idea of not having a selfish faith that just wants to benefit from God – like a rich kid who just sees her dad as an ATM. Instead I've been viewing it as a kind of a desire to get to know God and His nature – mostly so I can understand Him better and know what He wants me to do.

But this morning I had a flash of what it might really mean.

***

Before Aidan could walk or climb, he would look up at me with his adorable little face and say, "Uppee!" *(Up, please!)*

"Awww," I'd think, "He wants me to hold him!" So I'd pick him up with the intent to snuggle, but immediately he'd reach for something that he couldn't get to without my height/strength to get him there.

He wasn't seeking my face! He was seeking my hands. He was using me to get what he wanted.

Holland, on the other hand, would say, "Mommy, hodju!" *(Hold you!)* I'd pick her up, and her hands would go straight into my hair, where she'd just look at me and get her tactile fix (she loved to touch soft things), and enjoy the security of my arms.

This, I believe, is what it is to *seek His face.*

See, I'm such a practical person – I figured I was supposed to seek His face so I could be like Him and DO stuff for Him. This morning I realized that whether or not God chooses to do something for me with His hands, *above all* I should get my fix...my peace...my entire world of security and comfort from the fact that He is holding me in the security of His arms, and I can look into His face with complete trust that He is everything.

Not what He can *do*, but what He has *done* – what Jesus did so that we can simply be in God's presence.

There's no frantic reaching around to figure out all my needs and ask Him to meet them. He's already got it all covered. And I have no worries, because my eyes are on His face.

This old hymn came to my mind. It has new meaning for me today. Maybe it will for you, too.

Turn your eyes upon Jesus.

Look full in His wonderful face.

And the things of earth will grow strangely dim,

in the light of His glory and grace.[1]

Your face, Lord, will I seek.

---

[1]"Turn Your Eyes Upon Jesus". Lemmel, Helen. Public Domain

15

When I Didn't Get My Way

———————◆———————

Every now and then, my husband Eric asks me to speak in the weekend services at The Crossing.

It used to stress me out, but over the years and through God growing me into my sweet spot(s) of ministry, it is something I absolutely love to do.

We've been advertising the Baby Jesus series for Christmas for a while now, and I asked Eric if I could teach the "Everlasting Father" week. The fact that God is a Father to us has special meaning for me, and I just KNEW I was supposed to talk about it during the Christmas series. So many people don't have a positive father figure, and I was in danger of that myself as a child, but that's a story for another day.

Well, he had already talked to his dad (also a pastor) about teaching that weekend with him, but I begged him to let me do it instead. He agreed.

So over the past month, each time he's told The Crossing about the series, I've wondered if he's going to mention that his awesome wife Kelly is teaching that week.

He hasn't.

At Thanksgiving, I reminded him that he should let his dad know that he's off the hook for that weekend.

He didn't.

Last night he comes in our room and says, "My dad's been preparing to speak with me next weekend."

"Um. I thought you told him we changed our plans."

"I didn't. And honestly, Kelly, I really want to do this with my dad. It's a big deal to both of us."

PAUSE.

SIGH.

"OK."

Enter disappointment. *God, I was SO SURE You were going to use my talk to change MILLIONS OF LIVES through me! Or at least a few. I had such a great plan all worked out... I felt so GOOD about it. I thought You were with me on this! I felt the Spirit all over it! How dare Eric jack with what the Spirit clearly told me to do...*

I was at the intersection of self-pity and annoyance. Both roads were beneath my Royal Daughter-ness, but the pull was pretty strong.

Thankfully, in about two heartbeats, Jesus swooped in and pointed out a different path.

Twirl.

Oh. My. Word. It was for Twirl. That's why I hadn't gotten peace about my Twirl talk.

God gave me that message, not for The Crossing Church as a whole, but for the women of my church at my annual event. And the second I realized that, all the other fractured segments of Twirl that I was struggling to make cohesive came together. His plan unrolled like a red carpet across my mind.

He changed my plan. And made it better.

Life lessons learned from this experience:

1. Don't try to force my own agenda.

2. Don't get angry when my agenda gets changed. It just makes me look tacky and selfish. Take a deep breath and wait for the reveal.

3. In the meantime, keep believing that God is doing something behind the scenes – and He is WAY SMARTER than me.

You can make many plans, but the Lord's purpose will prevail. Proverbs 19:21

"For I know the plans I have for you," says the Lord. "They are plans for good and not for disaster, to give you a future and a hope." Jeremiah 29:11

16

Aunt Ginny's Sweet Potato Casserole

———◆———

My dad's sister Virginia (Aunt Ginny) always made Sweet Potato Casserole for holiday meals when I was a child. My mom got her recipe and started making it as well. It is literally the only way our family has ever eaten sweet potatoes (a.k.a. yams).

I've been sharing this with friends for years (including the time I made it for everyone to sample at a Twirl event). It has become widely requested by their families at holiday meals. I don't care if you don't like sweet potatoes. If you like pecans and brown sugar and butter, this will rock your world.

Ingredients
2 big cans yams, drained (29 oz. each) or equivalent fresh, cooked sweet potatoes, peeled.
1 stick butter, softened
1 tsp. vanilla
2 eggs
½ cup milk
½ tsp. cinnamon
½ tsp. nutmeg

1 cup sugar

Beat well (I use a mixer); pour into 9x13 baking dish. Sometimes I use a normal round casserole dish, but the larger pan allows for a greater topping-to-potato ratio.

Topping
1/2 cup brown sugar
1/3 cup butter
1 cup chopped pecans
Combine, microwave 'til butter is melted, stir, and spread over yam mixture.

Bake at 350° until bubbly (about 30-35 min).

Variations & Ideas
Make multiple little oven-proof dishes of this casserole, freeze them (uncooked), and bake for any old meal instead of waiting for a holiday.

Sometimes I bake them like that and give them to single friends who don't cook. If you do that, just don't expect to get your dish back.

Make way more topping than the recipe requires. It's the best part.

Put it in a Crock Pot if you need to free up oven space or want it done when you get home from work; cook till center is hot (you don't want raw eggs in the middle). The topping will not get crispy, so that's lame. If you have a removable crock, you could potentially put it in the oven under the broiler briefly to try to crisp it up. If you try that, let me know how it works.

17

Dangerous Blessing

———◆———

One day as Jesus was preaching on the shore of the Sea of Galilee, great crowds pressed in on him to listen to the word of God. He noticed two empty boats at the water's edge, for the fishermen had left them and were washing their nets. Stepping into one of the boats, Jesus asked Simon, its owner, to push it out into the water. So he sat in the boat and taught the crowds from there.

When he had finished speaking, he said to Simon, "Now go out where it is deeper, and let down your nets to catch some fish."

"Master," Simon replied, "we worked hard all last night and didn't catch a thing. But if you say so, I'll let the nets down again." And this time their nets were so full of fish they began to tear! A shout for help brought their partners in the other boat, and soon both boats were filled with fish and on the verge of sinking. Luke 5:1-7

Reading Luke Chapter 5 today. This is what I saw.

Jesus was preaching from a boat a little bit out from shore. He got done preaching and told Simon to move into deeper water and get some fish, presumably for dinner. (Notice this was in front of a crowd. He was done speaking, but He's a fascinating dude; I'm guessing people were still milling around, watching what was happening.)

Simon said, "Yeah, we already tried that, like all night long, and zippo. But, hey, if you say so..."

And then their nets filled up and started to rip! They were like, "Oh, CRAP!" And they had to call for help.

They got a blessing SO BIG that they weren't prepared to handle it. They had to call friends to come and take some. They didn't just *choose* to share the overabundant blessing; they were *forced* to!

This reminds me of the stories of the couple times Jesus miraculously multiplied food and fed large crowds. Ever notice that there were *always* leftovers?

Either Jesus sucks at calculating need, or He just loves to make a point about how much He wants to OVER-PROVIDE.

So both boats were over-filled, and they began to sink. Their blessing was so big, it became dangerous!

It was so big, it required faith in Jesus to SURVIVE IT!!!

I tell you what. This is written on my hand today: ASTONISH ME TODAY, JESUS!

I want to see a blessing so big that I am forced to share it with others. So big that it will require faith to survive it. Because Jesus doesn't want to just do something in my life that my own cleverness can accomplish; He wants to do something in my life that is so obviously from Him that I can't take personal credit. And so over-the-top that I won't have to decide whether or not to share; I won't have a choice. Abundance and gratitude will force me to call others to experience

Jesus the way I have.

What if you made that your prayer today? Too many Christians settle for claiming the promise in the verse below, but only focus on "needs"...

And this same God who takes care of me will supply all your needs from his glorious riches, which have been given to us in Christ Jesus. Philippians 4:19

...instead of including this promise, with a focus on "more"...

Now all glory to God, who is able, through his mighty power at work within us, to accomplish infinitely more than we might ask or think... Ephesians 3:20

Open up your mind to more than just getting your needs met, to the dangerous blessing God might have up His sleeve for you. And get ready to share.

18

On Striking Out Without Jesus

———————◆———————

John 6:16-18ish

That evening Jesus' disciples went down to the shore to wait for him.

(Waiting for Jesus to show up is not always super exciting, right?)

But as darkness fell and Jesus still hadn't come back...

(Waiting for Jesus to show up as life gets darker, scarier, lonelier... that's not so fun, either.)

...they got in the boat and headed across the lake.

(Oooh, you silly disciples. Instead of waiting a little longer, you shrugged your shoulders and struck out on your own.)

Soon a gale swept down upon them and the sea grew very rough...

(Yep. Take off without Jesus, and the storm will come. Count on it.)

And they rowed fruitlessly until Jesus met them in the storm and saved the day. I mean, saved the night.

I think this pretty much speaks for itself. But in case you missed it, keep waiting for Jesus, even when it's dark, and don't strike out on your own. Don't jump the gun or try to force something that isn't ready to happen. Life is so much harder when you're trying to row your boat alone.

Manipulating situations, convincing other people to help you, feeling the weight of the wanting and the pressure to get there all on your shoulders. And you row. And row. And it feels like you're getting nowhere.

Did you leave without Jesus?

If you already did, it's OK. He'll meet you in the storm.

I don't know about you, but I much prefer learning from the disciples' mistakes than my own. Have a quick look at your life. Where are you rowing and rowing and making no progress? Maybe it's time to rest and ask Jesus to help it happen when the time is right.

19

What We Can Live Without

———◆———

Blog Post December 11, 2011

I've been living without a clothes dryer since Thanksgiving.

It's funny how little this impacts my life.

It helps that my kids all wash their own clothes, so I'm not constantly faced with a mountain of laundry. I do help them hang their clothes up so they dry properly.

It helps that it's winter, so the house can use some extra moisture in the air.

It helps that we are OK with wearing jeans at least three times before we wash them.

It helps that I have a good washing machine, so it spins the clothes out well.

It struck me this morning that I'm not super bothered by this, and I was trying to figure out why. I guess that all of the above reasons tell you why.

Then it struck me that I lived without a microwave for about two years, after my friend died of cancer, and I got freaked out about the crack in the door of my microwave and the carcinogens that might have been leaking out and attacking us while we were waiting for our corn dogs to cook. I threw the microwave in the trash and was too busy enjoying the extra counter space in my little kitchen to want to buy another one.

We are living without the internet at home. We moved into the boondocks, and haven't done the work of figuring out what will work for us. Temporarily, we have a mobile phone hotspot that works. Sometimes. If you position the phone right and don't move. So besides our phones, we are living without the net.

Why am I sharing this with you? In our super-equipped, super-entitled culture, we get it into our heads that we are entitled to a certain level of living, and we refuse to make do or exercise self-discipline when our income doesn't support it.

Sometimes we lose access to or the use of something, and we freak out.

But sometimes when we think we need something, and we're forced to live without it, we simply adapt.

> *...for I have learned how to be content with whatever I have. I know how to live on almost nothing or with everything. I have learned the secret of living in every situation, whether it is with a full stomach or empty, with plenty or little. For I can do everything through Christ, who gives me strength. Philippians 4:11b-13*

You'd be surprised what you can live without. I am. And it makes me far more prone to gratitude when I receive blessings.

20

The Courage to Encourage

———◆———

This Sunday after church, a woman I didn't know came up to me and said, "Remember when I tithed?"

We pastor a large church and meet many people, so this kind of thing happens often. I scrambled around in my brain looking for a memory to connect with this woman, and (fortunately), it popped up.

Flashback two weeks...

She met me in the aisle after church. Her eyes were huge with tears. I saw fear combined with a soft heart, wanting to trust Jesus. She said, "Pastor Kelly, I really want to tithe, but if I do, I won't have enough money to pay my bills."

GULP. It takes courage to stand on a stage in front of hundreds of people and preach the concept of biblical tithing—giving back to God the first tenth of what He gives us. Looking into the eyes of someone who will genuinely not have what she needs if she tithes... that takes it to a whole new level.

I took a deep breath and said gently, "All I can tell you is what I believe to be true, and what I know from personal experience. If you do, God promises that He will take care of you. I don't know what else to say."

We stood there and I prayed boldly that God would bless her in unbelievable ways as she took that leap. As I walked away, I begged Him to show up in her life. I believe, but imagine the weight on my chest as I guide someone who is already lacking to make this sacrifice. I know He'll provide, but what if He waits awhile? "Oh, God, please come through..."

Back to Sunday. Smiling, she said, "I could hardly wait to come and tell you! I gave $80. $70 was tithe, and $10 was Samurai [our special giving campaign at the time]."

"Yeah?" I said. "Awesome!"

She continued, "And last week I was given $800."

No. Freakin'. Way.

Me: "Eight hundred dollars?!"

Laughing, she said, "Yes! That's 10 times what I gave! I had to come and tell you!"

"Thank you, Jesus!" I yelled. "Do you have any idea how hard it was for me to tell you to tithe?"

"Yeah," she said, "And you told me to 'do it anyway'. And I did."

And that's how God built my faith this weekend. He did it. He came through like He promised He would. That's our story, me and my new tithing buddy. Neither of us will ever forget it, and fear is struck down as the glory of our loving Father shines all over us.

When the Spirit of God prompts you to tell a friend to do the right thing, listen, OK? Because you might be in just the right place to help her walk into next-level faith and open up to more of God's blessing.

21

Vacation Brain

———————◆———————

I'm suffering from a condition that comes about when I'm on an extended time off from the daily routine. It's called Vacation Brain.

Wait, did I say "suffering"? Actually, I'm *thriving* on this condition. It's a state of mind. Actually, it's more a state of soul. And I like it.

And then I think, why can't I live with this condition every day of my life?

Vacation Brain every day.

Yes, please.

You're thinking I'm a little loopy. And maybe the combo of sun, a little wine and locally produced dried-fish spread on pita are affecting me. Along with these fresh Bing cherries I can't stop eating. (Can anyone read the word Bing without thinking of Chandler?)

But anyway, here are some of the symptoms that I'd like to take back home with me. Maybe you'll find it contagious and catch some of it yourself.

Symptoms of Acute Vacation Brain

On vacation, I spend time with Jesus. OK, I spend time with Jesus most mornings at home, but when there's no schedule to keep, the time is unhurried. I drink a lot (and I do mean *a lot*) of coffee and read, journal, pray, and talk with Eric about what I'm reading/thinking.

On vacation, I get to sit and talk with my husband for as long as I want. And I get to listen to what he's learning/thinking. If you know Eric, you know that's always fascinating. Back when we were newlyweds, I would always ask him on the way home from vacations, "How are we going to be different when we go home?" Sometimes we'd decide on vacation that we were going to look for a new job or ministry or place to live. I love change. I love improvement. And vacation seems like a great time to step back and have a look at my current place in life, and determine if any changes need to be made.

On vacation, I get to examine myself. Psalm 23 says, *He leads me beside still waters.* Back in "those" days, I'm guessing that still water was one of the only ways you could see a good reflection of yourself. God leads us to a restful place where we can examine ourselves.

He restores my soul comes next. On vacation, I can get a good look at myself and let God restore my soul to a healthy place during a time of rest. On this trip, Eric and I have had some – um – *energetic chats* about a blind spot in my life, that I am committing to change.

On vacation, I read. I read Scripture, I read books that inspire me and build my faith in Jesus, and I read fiction. This trip, I've read Pablo Giacopelli's *Holding on Loosely*, and I'm just finishing a second spiritual-growth book. Both of these books have brought us much healing and perspective as we've recently come out of a painful season in our life/ministry. I started reading a third faith-building book, but Eric just stole it from me. (In his defense, he is the one who bought it.) This morning I finished a novel I picked up for fifty cents at a flea market. It was pretty good. I do love to read fiction for fun. And I rarely do it. Except on vacation.

On vacation, we learn from the locals. The locals will tell you the best places to eat and the places to avoid. You can't always rely on reviews online, because generally the crabbiest people are the loudest. If you just look online, you'll think everywhere sucks. A nice local who actually knows the area will give you the truth. This is a good lesson for life. Ask someone who has intimate knowledge of something, and then go experience it and decide for yourself.

On vacation, we also learn from the experts. Yesterday we drove to a place called The Old Salty Dog to eat hot dogs, JUST because Adam Richman from *Man vs. Food* ate there and said it was awesome. It was. Another good lesson for life. Listen to the experts. But again, then you have to go experience it and decide for yourself.

On vacation, we actually look at each other and talk. All five of us. We sit and eat meals together. Sometimes we cook, sometimes we go out. But we don't have to run to the *next thing*. We enjoy our food slowly, and we talk and smile at each other. And we say *I love you* a lot. We don't have ringing phones and commute time and schedule-jamming requests. We have time to live together and love each other.

On vacation, we laugh. We're silly. My kids play together in the pool. My husband asks me if I dare him to jump into a private pool as we're walking back from the beach.

"NO!"

"Haha, I'm just kidding. Unless you say I can do it... then I totally will."

"Jeez... NO! You'll get arrested!"

On vacation, we sleep when we're tired, we wake when we're rested, and we eat when we're hungry. Natural rhythms that God created, not dictated by a clock or a culturally-acceptable timeframe.

On vacation, we seek to be healthy. OK, I know, we do that all the time. But it seems that on vacation, we have time and energy for an extra 10 push-ups or a little longer run. And we feel good about ourselves. We've also been careful this vacation to be strategic about what we eat so that we continue to feel good about ourselves. Hence, the bowl of cherries beside me.

On vacation, it's easier to not judge other people. Huh? Well, we're at the beach. At the beach, you see all shapes and sizes, ages, ethnicities, and economic levels. But we're all there for roughly the same purpose: to enjoy ourselves and appreciate God's creation. Who cares if there's cellulite? Who cares if there's no makeup? Who cares if your clothes are stained or you smell like sweat? It's VACATION! I won't judge you if you won't judge me.

What a lovely way to live.

On vacation, we use what we have. We wear what we packed. We make do with what we brought. I've been out of my Mary Kay moisturizing cream for a week, so I'm just using my daughter's body lotion until I can order more cream from my sister. Remarkably, I didn't immediately develop wrinkles, blotches, or zits. Also, I'm cooking in a tiny kitchen with a limited amount of supplies. Funny: I can get along just fine without a paring knife, wooden spoon, pizza stone, or much counter space. I made pecan pie in a rectangular cake pan. And it tasted GREAT! It's amazing what we think we need, and really don't.

On vacation, we don't stress out about being clean and organized. There are tiny ants marching around the kitchen, and I just don't really care. The only shower Aidan gets in is the one by the pool, and I just don't really care. The beds aren't made, and there's a pile of towels and damp, sandy clothing behind me by the door, and I just don't really care. I have more important things to worry about. Like sitting here listening to a Rick Riordan novel on CD with my kiddos.

On vacation, we no longer try to get more out of an experience than we should. (This is a newer philosophy for us.)

Consider this:

Have you ever stuffed yourself until you're in pain, just so you can get your money's worth at a buffet?

Have you ever exhausted yourself and your children just so you can get your money's worth out of an amusement park?

Have you walked until you're half-dead or stayed in the sun until you're burnt or stayed up late talking or partying until you are barely coherent and no longer having fun? And then you regret it the next day?

We've done all of these. And we just won't anymore. Instead, we take what there is to enjoy from an experience, and then let it go before we hate it.

For example, we were at an amusement park last week. We'd arranged to take the hotel shuttle back at 8:15 pm. But at 4:45, we were hot, sweaty, tired, and some of us had headaches. Rather than sticking it out to get our money's worth or soak up every possible second available to us, we made the wise choice to call for an earlier shuttle. We left while we were still enjoying ourselves. We went back to our hotel to cool off in the pool, and we ordered pizza. The amusement park, then, did not leave a bad taste in our mouths. Rather, we have memories of a lovely day that ended well.

At the beach this week, we aren't putting pressure on ourselves to spend all day, every day, in the waves. Rather, we're strategic about enjoying the beach, the pool, and the area. But we will not kill ourselves trying to see more, get more, eat more, do more. I think that old mindset is one of fear. *We'll NEVER get to do this again, so get all you can!* I prefer to trust that our good God will indeed provide another opportunity for enjoyment in the future. We are grateful for each opportunity we're given, and we're careful not to suck it dry or try to get more out of it than has been provided for us.

Well, I'm tired of writing (finally), and I'm on vacation, so I'm not going to try to make more of this than it is. But I'm happy to have gotten this on paper.

This Vacation Brain, vacation state of mind; I'd like to live this way at home, too.

Starting each day with Jesus.

Letting peace rule the day.

Loving my family well.

Living according to a natural rhythm.

Relaxing my expectations on myself and others.

Being content with what has been provided for me.

Living in gratitude.

Sounds good.

I'm going to the pool with my daughter.

And then to get ready for my date tonight with a really hot pastor. He's picking me up at 6:30.

22

Holland & Me

———————◆———————

Today is the first day of school for my two oldest kiddos.

Holland is entering 6th grade and her first year at this school. Yesterday as she lounged on the couch beside me while I attempted to beat my friend Tracy in Words With Friends, I asked Holland if she had picked out her outfit for the first day. She looked at me blandly and said, "No, Mom. If you try really hard on your first day of school, you'll look like you're...trying too hard."

Oh. Good to know.

This morning as we were driving to school, I looked over and asked Holland (who, amazingly, scored shotgun; this never happens, as Braden is always the first one ready), "Are you nervous?"

Holland: "No. *(duh)* I don't get nervous."

Me: (Preparing to give her a little "you're confident because you're God's girl, and He makes you strong and unconcerned about what other people think of you, etc." speech...) "You wanna know why you're not nervous?"

Holland: *(Matter-of-fact)* "Because I'm like you."

Whoa.

Now, it's important as a parent of a nearly-teenager that I *never* over-react, positively or negatively, to *anything*, lest she slam shut the door of her heart/mood/emotion, so, very calmly, I made our "face" (we did matching duck lips before they were cool) and said: "Totally."

And we fist-bumped.

I guess she *is* kinda like me. That's cool.

Hey, moms: our daughters will model what they see in us. The positives, the negatives, the neutrals… It looks like they're ignoring us, but I promise you they're catching way more than we realize.

There's so much of myself that I'd like to improve. So today I'm inspired to be the woman I want my daughter to grow up and become. I'm challenging you to do the same.

Even if you can't twirl for yourself, twirl for *her.*

23

Grace For All

—————◆—————

It was Aidan's second day of school. He was 10. He's a pure creative, which means that organization is very low on his priority scale, but optimism is high, so our conversation went something like this:

Me: "Did you remember your guitar?"

Aidan: *(pause. pause.)* "Noooo..."

Me: "You have a lesson after school today. Dude! *(Sigh)*"

Aidan: "It's ok! There are tons of guitars at church. I'll borrow one."

***

That was half of our conversation that morning. Here's the other half of it; the part that came first:

Aidan (as he gets in the van): "I can't find my backpack."

Me: "Did you leave it at church yesterday?"

Aidan: "Maybe."

[Insert guitar conversation here.]

Aidan: "After we drop Braden and Holland off, can we please stop at church on the way to school? I need my math book, and it's in my backpack! And my homework! It's done, but it's in my backpack!"

Note to reader: THIS IS THE SECOND DAY OF SCHOOL.

Me: *(another sigh)* "I don't know. We have to pick your friend up, and I don't want to be late."

And then, like the cherry on top of my early-morning stress sundae, I hear a pleasant little "Bing!" My low fuel light is blinking. The gauge is on empty. And it's a roughly 35-minute drive to Aidan's school. Jesus, help me.

No, for real. *Jesus, help me.*

So I start thinking and praying. Is this how we want to start our school year? Making allowances for his irresponsibility? We've gone through so many lunch boxes and mittens and shoes and socks and hair brushes over the years because he Leaves Stuff Everywhere.

Do I help him out today so he doesn't have to stay in for recess, or do I let him suffer the consequences of his being... himself?

If I let the natural consequences take their course, maybe he'll learn his lesson.

But... grace.

[Insert Jesus-please-miraculously-stretch-my-gas-supply prayer here.]

Me: "Fine, Aidan, we'll stop at the church."

***

We take a detour, and I unlock the church door for him and return to the van. A minute later, he comes back out, with his classic "dejected" stance. Arms hang limply, eyes on the ground, despair oozing from his pores.

"It's not there."

Me: "Did you check my office? The LIT room?, etc."

Him: "Yes. It's not there. I think it might be in the closet in the mudroom at home."

I can feel my nostrils flaring as I bite my tongue.

For the first time in human history, he has put his backpack AWAY, where it's supposed to go.

And then he couldn't find it.

I am going to die before I turn 40.

***

Sometimes when we choose to give someone grace, we fear that they'll never learn their lesson.

I told my Grandpa this past week that Eric has been preaching hard-core grace over the last few weeks. First thing Grandpa said?

"Too much grace is a license to sin."

Hmmm.

Yeah, I've heard that.

But GOD can do whatever He wants to grow and guide people into living out their true potential as He's created them. We don't have to be the rule-enforcers. We don't have to put limits on God's grace to try to keep people in line. We are called to give grace.

And *grace does the work* of changing people.

> *For the **grace** of God that brings salvation has appeared to all men. **[Grace] teaches us to say "No" to ungodliness and worldly passions,** and to live self-controlled, upright and godly lives in this present age, while we wait for the blessed hope—the glorious appearing of our great God and Savior, Jesus Christ, who gave himself for us to redeem us from all wickedness and to purify for himself a people that are his very own, **eager to do what is good.** Titus 2:11-14 (NIV, emphasis mine)*

Grace teaches people to choose not to sin. The grace of Jesus Christ makes people eager to do what is good. With grace, He brings the purification. The desire to live right.

Condemnation never made anyone feel empowered to live right.

I had a choice that morning. I could leave Aidan to the consequences of his plight, or I could try to help him. I could give grace. I gave grace, and (that day, at least), God chose to let him deal with the consequences. Even as a mother, I can choose grace and trust that God will teach my child in His own way.

Give somebody His grace today. It'll be the best thing that could ever happen to them.

Receive His grace today. It'll be the best thing that ever happened to you.

Let His grace teach you to say "no" to sin. It's not your self-discipline or self-condemnation that will change you. It's His grace. It will make you *eager to do what is good,* even when it's not natural.

Now I need to go downstairs to the lobby and find Aidan's guitar. Because I just remembered he left it here after his lesson yesterday. *(sigh)*

P.S. As I drove and prayed that morning, I watched my gas gauge rise to 1/8 tank. And the low fuel light went off.

Grace.

24

Impatient Me

———◆———

In our church bathrooms, we have automatic, motion-sensored paper towel dispensers.

I do NOT like waiting for that stupid paper towel to dispense.

So I have a strategy. It's called

1. Flush toilet.

2. Wave hand in front of dispenser.

3. Wash hands.

4. Rip off towel that was dispensing while I was busy washing my hands.

Bing. Bang. Boom. Done.

It's a good strategy when I remember to do it in that order. When I forget and reverse steps 2 and 3, I have to stand there and WAIT at LEAST 2.5 seconds for the dispenser to do its work before I can dry my drippy hands. And I'm annoyed. Never mind that the dispenser does all the work, and all I have to do is watch as it gently presents the paper towel to me.

Never mind that what I previously had to accomplish through my own strength is now accomplished for me. Instead, I'm annoyed because I. want. that. paper. towel. NOW.

Impatient me.

I overlook the blessing and ease freely offered, and instead get an attitude because it doesn't come fast enough. I almost think I'd be happier cranking the towel out myself instead of waiting for it, because at least that way I feel like something's being accomplished.

Oh, God, I do this to You, too.

You have taught me that You want to take care of stuff for me.

But often this means waiting a bit.

And very often, I'd rather just crank something out in my own strength rather than waiting for you to just ease it into place for me to receive and use.

Sigh.

Silly, impatient me.

25

&@%# Autocorrect

———◆———

I'm a firstborn. A type-A, dominant sanguine, who scores high on control. Thank JESUS for the fruit that the Spirit grows in me, to keep me from driving everyone nuts with my control-freakishness.

This has been a profoundly busy week. Two weeks, actually. School Christmas concerts, Twirl, illness, work, and the always-taxing multi-service weekends at The Crossing. I have not taken as much time as usual to create the space I need to tune in to the Holy Spirit's restraint in my life. The beauty of what the Holy Spirit does (when I let Him), is that He softens me, gives me the capacity to be gentle, loving, sympathetic, patient, and accepting of everyone – especially those I love most – just how they are!

The famous "Love Chapter" in the Bible, 1 Corinthians 13, says *love believes the best.* Meaning, when you live as a carrier of God's love, you believe the best about people: their intentions, their behaviors. When you hear gossip that's negative, you just say, "I won't believe that. I believe the best about that person." Love believes the best. When your family member frustrates you, you choose to believe that they didn't do it on purpose. They just forgot again.

Recently I saw a quote from author/speaker Lisa Bevere. She said, "*Love believes the best* is very different from *love demands the best.*"

Daaaang. Way too often I place super high expectations on my family, and they don't live up to those expectations. Then instead of believing the best about them (assuming they love me and want to help me and are doing the best they can), I get frustrated with them and demand more and correct more.

Over the last two days, I've been increasingly aware of my *Autocorrect* working overtime. Meaning, I *automatically correct* my husband, my kids, and anyone else unlucky enough to be around me, if they do or say something that I find incorrect or unacceptable. *Dang Autocorrect.* Autocorrect flies directly in the face of Autoaccept, which is what we're called to do for others since Jesus did it for us.

Therefore, accept each other just as Christ has accepted you so that God will be given glory. Romans 15:7

Autocorrect instead of Autoaccept is a symptom of a bigger problem: failing to accept myself. To believe the best about myself instead of just shouldering more demands. Accept my flaws, accept what I can't change, accept that my energy is limited, and accept that what's best for me isn't always what other people want. I must make time for myself. To be healthy and live at peace so I can accept others and love them well.

Make time for myself sounds selfish, doesn't it? It inspires images of bubble baths, wine, chocolate, indulgence... and we think, *how selfish.* But the truth is that when we get off the crazy train and be still for a few minutes, we make space to feel God soothe our frazzled hearts, to hear His correction and get our hearts uncluttered. As we let His grace cover where we've gone astray, his peace moves in, and we are renewed in our minds.

So today I'm doing that. I'm home alone. And I'm creating space to hear God so I can shut off Autocorrect, Autoannoy, Autocranky, and all their cousins... and instinctively go for Autograce and Autoaccept, because that's what's been given to me.

26

What Works For Me

———◆———

What works for me is a phrase I've learned to use instead of *this is the right way to do it.*

It adds a little humility to this firstborn's perfectionism.

And, well, it's generally more accepted by most people. Particularly my husband when he's loading the dishwasher.

Try it. People might like you better.

It works for me.

27

A Trip Home

———◆———

This weekend, I was in Alabama.

I was at my home church (where my family went during my last two years of high school and beyond) for a memorial service on Saturday and church Sunday.

I think I was given at least 82 hugs. Southern people hug.

I heard a lot of, "remember me?" and, "you're pretty!" Southern people are really, really nice.

I was also told, "I didn't know your momma and daddy had another daughter!" (Thanks, Mom.) In their defense, I have been gone a long time.

I realized it is quite difficult to participate in any type of food-fast when one is home for a visit in Alabama. I was able to resist the sausage biscuits but not the bread pudding. I recalled my husband/pastor saying, "If you want to break your fast while you're down there, go ahead," so I thanked Jesus for bread pudding and ate some. It was awesome. The sauce has apricot brandy in it. When Mom bought that brandy, it was the first (and probably will be the only) time I've ever seen my mother buy alcohol. Weird.

I also bought and ate boiled peanuts from a Crock Pot in a gas station. Be still my soul. If you are a northerner who has not tried boiled peanuts, look in the canned vegetable section of your local Walmart. Warm them up in the microwave a bit before you eat them. It's not exactly the same thing, but you'll get the delicious sodium-laden idea.

My sister Chrissie had some fun with a tail from a *deceased cat* (she works at a vet clinic). When I had my back turned (I had gone to say hi to the bunny who lives in the garage), she put that tail under her truck tire. As I walked back up, she had a horrified expression on her face and yelled, "I THINK I KILLED THE CAT!" My heart stopped, and all I could think was, *what if it's not totally dead?* When Chrissie burst out laughing, and I saw the medical tape on the stub of the tail, I nearly killed her.

I also nearly killed my dad when he handed me a bag of pecans (as in, they went pecan-picking), with a HUGE fake palmetto bug in it. (For the uninitiated, a palmetto bug is like a giant roach.) Hardy-har-har-har. He then toured the kitchen, looking for the best place to hide it to scare my sister Katie. He picked behind the honey bear, and she did find it, but she didn't react much. Take THAT, Dad.

My Dad got a kick (no pun intended, till I saw the pun) out of making fun of my shoes. I, in turn, made fun of him as much as possible about anything I could come up with.

He ticked Katie off when he said she uses too much hot water when she showers.

My mother and Katie are both "Mary Kay Ladies", so I got plenty of advice about my *wrinkles*. They call them *expression lines*. How fancy.

We fought (and I really do mean *fought*) over the Ferrero Rocher chocolates Dad had. Did you know they make coconut ones? But the chocolate is white, so... yuck. White chocolate should not be a thing.

I was forced (by my mother) to play her keyboard and sing old hymns and camp tunes.

We told funny stories and laughed and laughed and laughed. We found out Katie didn't know about the little arrow lights that tell you which way an elevator is going. (Don't judge; our town doesn't even have a STOP LIGHT.)

We stayed up way too late. I slept on my nephew Ethan's loft bed and got to meet the lizard and the turtle. I told Ethan stories about the old days when his bedroom was mine, and that one time the camel cricket woke me up... shuffling around in my hair.

We stood on the bluff and looked over the valley and I just wanted to stay there because of all the places I've lived in my life (eight states), that one is really home. I would have taken pictures of my mountain, but pictures never do it justice, so I don't try anymore.

The trip happened because of Mrs. Linda Drake, who went to heaven right after Christmas after a battle with breast cancer. Her older daughter, Lisa, was in my wedding, and I was in hers. Mr. and Mrs. Drake have been my parents' best friends forever. Chrissy and Ryan, the two younger kids, used to play and fight with my sisters Katie and Chrissie. They're family to us, no matter where we roam.

We spent two hours on Saturday praising God for her life. Being happy for her but sad for us, a church full of people who loved Mrs. Drake. People whose lives she touched. People she served. Marriages she helped save, girls she ministered to when they were in a bad place. A bunch of us she fed when she was camp cook at Ponderosa Bible Camp. Lots of us "rose and called her blessed". I would like to think I could leave a legacy like that. I do hurt for her family. And for Mr. Drake. But God is still good.

One last thing. Southern people can SANG. Granted, the music in my home church is not like what I'm used to now. And I do love The Crossing's worship. But in that little Alabama church, with those five singers up there – every one of 'em could place that harmony just right.

And when we stood at the end of the service and sang "It is Well With My Soul," with my sisters and my mom and Anna, a truly professional singer, standing beside me, it was like heaven came down. I wanted to cry but couldn't, because that would've messed up my voice, and it was just too incredible to get to sing together just like old times, the reason we have hope:

When peace like a river attendeth my way
When sorrows like sea billows roll
Whatever my lot, Thou hast taught me to say, "It is well, it is well with my soul."
My sin--oh, the bliss of this glorious thought--my sin, not in part, but the whole
Is nailed to the cross, and I bear it no more!
Praise the Lord! Praise the Lord, oh, my soul!
And Lord, haste the day when my faith shall be sight.
The clouds be rolled back like a scroll.
The trump shall resound and the Lord shall descend!
It is well, it is well with my soul![1]

And that's the part where my conservative, reserved Daddy cut loose with a yell because that's the truth. That's the hope. That's the part that keeps us all bound together as family and keeps us from falling apart alone. This life isn't all there is. Because of the cross and the hope of the future, we keep living and twirling and dreaming and praying and telling people about Jesus. And when we go meet Him, on our final trip Home, well, that's just the icing on the cake.

---

[1]"It is Well With My Soul", Spafford, Horatio. Public Domain

28

Thank-Yous 101

———◆———

I looked at Eric today across the lunch table, pen in my hand poised over a really sweet note card. I say really sweet, because it's all soft and fabric-feeling, instead of thin and glossy. I paid a little bit for this box of cards. They are gorgeous. I'm going to have to write my friend Kelsey a note on one of them, because I KNOW that the moment she gets her fingers on it, she'll rub it on her cheek, delighting in the texture. It's true. I'll give you fifty bucks if she doesn't.

Anyway, I looked at Eric and said, "I love writing thank-you notes." Then I backpedaled very quickly before God struck me with lightning for lying. "I mean, I *hate* writing thank-you notes, but I enjoy coming up with the right words."

My grandpa used to say, "If I can take the time to send you money, you can take the time to write a thank-you note." He also said, "If you can put your feet under my [dinner] table, you can help around the farm." But that doesn't have anything to do with anything at the moment. His point was, if someone can take the time or effort to do something nice for you, the very least you can do is write a simple little note of thanks.

So thank-you notes are part of my life. A BIG part of my life.

I suppose if God would quit sending awesome people around me – blessing me through them – I wouldn't have to write so many thank-yous.

We require that all our Crossing Church staff write at least 4 thank-you notes every Wednesday. A culture of gratitude comes along with a culture of honor. Sometimes people will say, "I don't know what to write." So here are a couple of tips.

• Be specific. "Thank you for the wedding gift," is nowhere near as personal as, "Thank you for the salsa maker."

• Don't be too specific. "Thank you for the $40 check," is not super cool. It's better to be a little more vague with monetary gifts. "Thank you for the wedding gift," is more appropriate then.

• Mention what the gift/blessing/assistance meant to you. "It's really nice," is not as meaningful as, "We look forward to making gallons and gallons of salsa with it." "Thanks for your help," is fine, but "Your wisdom is valuable beyond words," is ooh, so much nicer.

• Don't grovel. "I can't believe you'd be so nice to me. I totally don't deserve a new salsa maker," is tacky. If you must make a point about being humbled by a gift, just say something like, "I'm honored that you would be so kind," or if it's a really big deal, maybe, "I'm completely overwhelmed that you would be the hands and feet of Jesus in such a generous way."

• Don't go on about a payback. "I know I can never repay you for blah blah blah," isn't classy. A gift isn't given with the anticipation of a payback.

• Give a gift. Don't send a gift to say thanks for a gift. But if someone has blessed you with a favor or service such as time, wisdom, counsel, babysitting, or a meal, it shows honor to give a gift. Don't worry if the gift isn't of equal value of what they offered. Do something thoughtful, from the heart. Starbucks is a good choice. I mean, for some people...

Also, it's OK to say, "Please let me know if I can ever reciprocate." (But don't say that if you don't mean it.)

• I like to wrap it up with a prayer (something we can ALL offer). "I pray that God shows you His favor today in a special way." And then, *don't forget to actually pray.*

• Finish well. If you want to end with, "God bless you," be sure you don't overuse the word "bless/blessing/blessed" earlier in the note. There's nothing wrong with the classic, "Sincerely," or "Most sincerely." "Warm regards," is kind of formal. "Blessings," is OK. "MUAH!" is my lighthearted kiss-blowing for girl notes. Be yourself all the way to the end, so they close the card with a smile.

So I wrote my note. And I resisted the impulse to gush on and on about how wonderful these people are and how much they blessed us beyond what we'd *ever* feel worthy of, or how our life and ministry will be forever impacted by what we learned. Because sometimes, (in thank-you notes *and* some conversations, I've found), fewer words are better. Brief, classy, well-thought, full of weight and meaning. I added a gift. And I prayed that God would bring them a blessing in return.

Gratitude is integral to a life of faith. Noticing blessings will prepare you to receive more.

OK, now – before you forget – grab a pen and paper, and write someone a thank-you note.

29

Marriage and Freaks

———◆———

This morning as we sat in bed having our coffee and attempting a quiet time with Jesus (I say *attempting* because neither of us are super quiet), I told Eric something perplexing about myself, and finished with, "...I don't know; I'm a freak."

He looked back at me, super straight-faced, and said, "Yes. Yes, you ARE a freak."

Startled, I burst out laughing. And then he did, too, a little awkwardly. And then we had to process why that felt so weird. It's because he NEVER, EVER, EVER says anything like that to me.

I thought it was hilarious, because that's my kind of sense of humor. He did not, because it's not his. He doesn't "bust on" me like that. It feels wrong to him, and in his mind, his value and love for me precludes that kind of joking. He actually felt a little bad because he called me a freak! Does that sound weird to you? It might. But that's how our relationship functions.

It reminded me of a conversation I had with a friend the other day. She mentioned that her marriage *does* include that kind of jesting. A well-meaning associate, before he got to know her and her husband, attempted a bit of an *I'm concerned* conversation with her about her marriage. He literally thought they were struggling because their marriages functioned differently.

She was totally confused and said, "Um, I think we're pretty happy..."

Which reminded me of another conversation I had with Eric a few years into our marriage. We were *sooooo* happy and had *nooooo* conflict, and we thought *eeeeveryone's* marriage should look just like ours. Were just a little judgy about people who didn't get along the same way we did. And then we realized that couples have to do *what works for them.*

Every marriage has its functions and dysfunctions. It's not our place to pass judgment on someone else's marriage just because it doesn't function like ours. Actually, it's not our place to pass judgment on anyone else, period. John 14:1-5 tells us to accept each other and not to condemn people who don't live the same way we do.

We're to give grace to all people, both individually and in terms of how their relationships look.

After all, we are *all* freaks in some way or other, and that's what makes the love of God for us so very beautiful. And our love for each other even in spite of (or because of) our freakiness is pretty great too.

30

In Case You Need This Today

———————◆———————

As for me, I look to the Lord for help. I wait confidently for God to save me, and my God will certainly hear me. Micah 7:7

Scripture is full of verses that talk about looking to God for help and waiting confidently for Him.

Waiting *confidently*. As if you *know* He is scheduled to arrive.

Kind of like taking your garbage to the curb, and waiting *confidently* for the truck to pick it up. It has come before. It's scheduled to show. You don't stress about it. You just put your stuff out there and wait for it to be taken care of.

Put your stuff out there for Him today. He'll take care of it.

Hang in there.

31

And Aidan Said, "Duck."

———◆———

Tonight Eric and I let our kiddos watch the 90 minutes of footage we got from producer Mark Burnett, of The History Channel's upcoming *BIBLE* series. We worked our way through the Old Testament, answering our kiddos' questions and explaining some of the stories. Since this is unfinished footage designed to give pastors a feel for the series (so we can promote it), there are abrupt jumps from scene to scene, but some play out and are very powerful.

I sat on the couch between Holland and Aidan. We've been gone from our children all week, so Aidan (age 10) was feeling a little snuggly tonight. He was holding my hand, which I know won't last very long, so I was feeling grateful to be with my kiddos and grateful to God for the opportunity to watch the Bible unfold in front of us and spark conversations. It's another way that we can inspire our children toward faith.

After experiencing Jesus' struggle on the road to the cross, we moved ahead to Mary finding Jesus' tomb empty and the skeptical Peter and John going back to look with her. They returned to the house with the rest of the disciples, where they gathered around a table, having bread and wine and speaking of Jesus being alive.

And Jesus appeared in the doorway. It was a beautiful moment as He slowly walked into the room, the awe spreading over the faces of the men who minutes ago had thought their Leader dead. The disbelief showed on Thomas' face, and we knew he would soon experience a powerful exchange of doubt for faith.

Jesus stepped into the room and placed his hand on Peter's head. Peter's eyes close, and our eyes welled with tears as we felt his emotion. Jesus moved to the next disciple, placing His hand on his head...

...and Aidan said, "Duck."

Jesus stepped around the circle of His disciples, placing His hand on the head of the next one...

...and Aidan said, "Duck."

Nail-scarred hand on precious head.

"Duck... Duck..."

And we all cracked up. A powerful moment of gratitude that our Leader is alive changed to imagining Him playing, "Duck, Duck Goose"[1] with His friends.

I bet Jesus would have thought that was pretty funny, too.

[1] Inexplicably, this game is called "Duck, Duck, Gray Duck" in Minnesota.

32

I'm So Vain, I Probably Think
They're Thinking About Me

◆————————

A couple years ago, we had recently hired a staff member. I didn't yet "get" this person's personality and communication style, so I was wondering about them. Here's the conversation I had with Eric:

Me: "I really don't know what X thinks of me. I just can't tell. I really feel like they don't like me very much. Or at least they think…" [I proceeded to ruminate on their opinion of me.]

Eric: "Hon. I'm not trying to be mean, but I just really don't think X thinks about you at all."

OUCH.

Heart check.

Too often we modify our behavior or choices or words or (at the very least) waste our brainpower worrying about what someone else is thinking about us. When in reality, they probably AREN'T.

Because in the real world (you know, instead of the one in our heads where everyone is consumed with US), everyone is actually consumed with what everyone else thinks of THEM. It's a manic, pointless cycle of fear rooted in pride.

What if we all just worried about what God thinks of us and stopped worrying about the opinions of others? Pastor Craig Groeschel is known for saying, *Worrying about what others think of you is the fastest way to forget what God thinks of you.*

God is awesome and creative, and He intentionally made us all in a brilliant variety. So be YOU.

Wear the shoes. (I'm still kicking myself for not wearing the white ones when I was in the mood, even though it was pre-Memorial Day. Who really would have cared? No one. NO ONE.)

Choose the career. (If you love it, someone might pay you to do it!)

Start the business. (Who knows? You might actually succeed. And what if you don't? Well, then you have no business, which is where you are today.)

Love your spouse. (Publicly. Never speak negatively about him. Brag to the world how awesome he is.)

Thrive in your body. (So WHAT if you're curvy? Oprah's curvy. She's done OK for herself.)

Be weird, if that's how you are.

Be shy, if that's how you are.

Be creative. Be silly. Be serious. Read books. Sing karaoke. Write poems. Paint stuff. Wear holey jeans. Paint your nails purple. Never wear a lick of makeup. Do math. Work out.

Live a focused, intense life.

Stop and smell the roses/coffee/chai/whatever.

Bleed and sweat for a calling.

Don't give a damn what other people think.

Give a damn what God does.

Live a life that is holy, pure, Spirit-led, loving, accepting, intentional, worthy of the title *God's Child.*

But do it with YOUR style, because your style is God's tool to change the world.

33

Having What it Takes

————◆————

I didn't mean to be a mom.

Initially, I mean. It was the weekend I turned 21 years old; I'd been married less than two years. We returned from a trip to LA for a friend's wedding, and I took a pregnancy test. *Surely not. But...?*

I took the test, set it down, and began the longest 30-second wait of my life. Just then, the door buzzed. The UPS guy was delivering a package to our apartment. By the time Eric retrieved the package, two very distinct lines showed on the stick thingy.

Holy moly. I was pregnant.

I've NEVER been one of those women who said, "I want a baby! I want kids!" I hated babysitting. I didn't (still don't) really enjoy other people's kids.

I was going to have a kid of my own. Braden was born in April, and he was the coolest little person ever. So easy to deal with. So much fun. So smart. Everybody liked him. He (being his mother's son) was famous for correcting the pronunciation of dinosaur names as people read him his Dino books.

A few years later, we had Holland. I had been coaching competitive cheerleading for a couple years, so when I found out she was a girl, I was like, "Noooooo!" I'd already had enough girl drama. But Holland was adorable. She had Shirley Temple ringlets.

Twenty months later, along came Aidan, followed swiftly by a vasectomy. Aidan's name means *fiery one*. He's a rock star with more ambition than anyone else I know, including his dad.

When Aidan was born, we were living about 35 minutes away from where Eric was living out his workaholism as a youth pastor. He rarely took a day off. I was very happy but kind of on my own. Two weeks into being a mother of three, I realized *I do NOT have what it takes to do this mom thing. I am going to lose my mind.*

Do you suspect that you don't *have what it takes* to live out the calling on your life right now? Whether it's motherhood or a career change or a relational struggle or caring for an elderly parent, do you constantly feel in the pit of your stomach that uncomfortable sensation that any moment you might lose your grip?

That was me. That's still me, sometimes, when I forget that I have the solution. This is what I decided to do, all those years ago, when I had one kindergartner and two kids in diapers. I started getting up at 5:30 to spend time alone with God. I hate mornings with a green passion, but I made a decision to get up every day *before the kids* and spend time re-focusing on who I am in the eyes of my Good Father before I lost myself in who I had to be for my world.

That's where I found the strength and wisdom and grace to do what I needed to do. Long before I learned the concept of spotting while twirling through life, I knew the solution to at least *starting* each day with a hope of success. It's time with God.

It set me up to live purposefully instead of victimish-ly.

I choose *to do today to the best of my ability with strength that comes from a Higher Power.*

I am not *a victim of my circumstances.*

My entire life has led up to this day, and I will seize it with confidence.

This morning-with-God habit has continued for years, and it's the #1 piece of advice I have for anyone who wonders *do I have what it takes to survive this season?* Get a fresh batch of wisdom and mercy straight from your Creator first thing every morning.

If you need wisdom, ask our generous God, and he will give it to you. James 1:5

The faithful love of the Lord never ends! His mercies never cease. Great is his faithfulness; His mercies begin afresh each morning. Lamentations 3:22-23

34

Potatoes, Kraut & Sausage

———————◆———————

This is Mrs. Foshee's recipe. Her son Jason was one of my good buddies in elementary and junior high. My mom wrote it out on a 3x5 card for me when I was newly married. I still have the card. She listed all the ingredients, and then wrote, "For time and temp, call mom!"

My family loves this meal, and it's great for those days when you want dinner ready when you get home. Braden requested it for his birthday one year, and his teenage friends all loved it. It doesn't matter if you don't like sauerkraut. The flavors all blend together, and it is *awesome*. You can adjust the amounts to feed 50 people, if you want. I've done that too.

Ingredients
1 lb. Polish sausage (like Hillshire Farms kielbasa), cut into bite-sized slices
Several peeled, cut potatoes
1 sliced white or yellow onion
1 can sauerkraut (including the juice)
1 can of cream-of-something soup OR homemade white sauce[1]
Sprinkle of salt & pepper
8 oz. pepper jack cheese, shredded

Instructions

Combine everything *except the cheese* in a Crock Pot, and cook on high for a couple hours or low if you start it in the morning and want it for supper. It's done when the potatoes are soft. Stir in cheese just before serving. I like to eat it with ketchup, but I'm weird.

[1]For homemade white sauce, see Chapter 64.

35

Just A Normal Day

———◆———

I spoke at church this past weekend. In preparation for preaching, I prayed more than I ever have before. Not that I don't usually pray, but lately God's been doing some really amazing stuff through prayer (including answering "yes" to the most trivial prayers). And He's doing stuff we can't accomplish on our own.

So despite a busy week in the office and less time than usual set apart for writing/studying, I prayed more. Rather than building myself up with more study and writing notes and going over what I planned to say, I went instead with the instruction given in Scripture.

"...build yourselves up in your most holy faith and pray in the Holy Spirit." Jude 1:20

I guess I figured if I had some time, I'd be better off asking the power of God to download everything I need instead of trying harder in my own power. So I prayed. A lot.

***

This morning, I was beginning Just a Normal Day.

And I thought, *Why on earth don't I pray just as intensely on Just a Normal Day?*

I mean, think about it. Your life is made up of Normal Days. There's only the occasional Big Opportunity like I had this weekend. And if you were to mess up your Big Opportunity, well, it's just one event.

On the other hand, Normal Days have far more capacity for awesome or awful.

Decisions you make, words you say, thoughts that develop attitudes and play out in habits...

Normal Day-in and Day-out make up the real whole of your life. A whole lot of little errors on Normal Days have the potential to be way more damaging than one fat blunder on a Big Opportunity. "Death by a thousand paper cuts," they say.

Why, oh, why, wouldn't we pray just as fervently – or more – on our Normal Days? Is it because with a Big Opportunity, we could fail in front of lots of people and change their opinions of us?

Really, if we think about it, our Normal Days add up to affect generations. We really don't want to mess that up.

So I'm upping my prayers. I'm challenging you to do the same. Let's ask God to download everything we need for our Normal Days so the *whole* of our lives are infused with His power – not just our Big Opportunities.

Never stop praying. 1 Thessalonians 5:17

36

The Soufflé Story

———◆———

It was 7:50 am, and we had just dropped Braden off at school. Staff meeting didn't start till 9, so we had more than an hour available to us. We decided to go to Panera for coffee. We generally don't eat breakfast that early, but faced with Panera's dazzling array of yummies, we chose a sausage & Gouda soufflé to snack on. Low carb, since we're making an effort to slim down a bit.

We filled our coffee cups and settled into a booth. With only one fork, we casually took turns picking away at the soufflé. For years, I've struggled with sharing food with my husband. Here are the reasons: He doesn't pay a lot of attention to his food, and he eats quickly. This means he gets more than me, and he will mindlessly finish whatever we're sharing, leaving me with (what I perceive) is *not enough.*

A few times we've had conversations about this. I have learned to strategically divide the food and get my own plate so I can eat slowly instead of competing with him and failing to enjoy my food. I've even told him that the sign of true love is handing the last bite of something you really like to the person you love. (Meaning, he should give it to me. Rarely does it go the other way. Huh.)

Back to the soufflé. With about a 2-inch piece left, he pushed the plate away, making a dismissive gesture, leading me to believe he was finished. I didn't think much about it, but subconsciously assumed the rest was for me to finish. I let it sit there, a little slice of God's goodness available to me when I'm ready to reach for it. I'm a delayed-gratification person.

And a minute later, he *(totally unaware!)* grabbed it and popped all but a tiny crust in his mouth. He caught my look and handed me the half-inch crust, smiling because he thought he was being nice by giving me the last bite. But... but... it wasn't the good bite I was looking forward to! It was a crumb! And he'd done it again: managed to offend me by eating "my" food.

Of course, I had to say something about it. *WHY must I always talk?* I should have smiled and said thank you.

But I (slightly offended) said, "Hey! I thought that was mine!"

"Huh?" He had no idea.

"Yeah. You pushed it away. I was saving it!"

Well, he felt bad and gave me the sad lower lip, and I immediately regretted saying anything. He's a sweetheart, and he didn't mean to be insensitive. I apologized for making him feel bad, and the moment passed, but it reminded me of something I've been reading/thinking about lately.

What's the mindset that causes me to be frustrated when he takes "my" bite?

A poverty mindset. A poor-girl mentality.

I'll never get a taste of this ever again. There's not enough for both of us. I have to hold on to my "treat". In a few minutes (or days), I'm going to need to feed myself or treat myself, and – God forbid – I won't have what I need.

My word. The soufflé is $3.99. I can go buy another one. I can go buy six.

Why am I concerning myself with the crumbs like some kind of peasant girl, when I'm backed by the Royal Treasury? Not just in Panera today, but in life.

It's a food issue.

It's a money issue.

It's a time issue.

It's a "my stuff" issue.

It's a whatever-I-think-I-have-or-might-need issue.

It's not new. I've preached and written about it before.

But it's a THING that affects SO MANY of us.

We're royalty. Kids of the KING, who assures us we're loved - He already gave up His most prized possession, *Jesus,* in order to pay for our adoption into His family! How much more will He make sure we have the simple things like food, clothes, car, home, joy, peace, chocolate...

Since he did not spare even his own Son but gave him up for us all, won't he also give us everything else? Romans 8:32

Why do we insist on holding onto what we think will make us feel good?

Why do we refuse to share? Why do we freak out when someone else takes what we think should be ours? Why do we eat and eat and eat or hoard or hide out of fear that we'll never get good things EVER again?

If we have our daily bread today (He says He'll provide it), why not assume He'll provide it again tomorrow?

A pauper mentality. I struggled with it much of my life. God has broken it in me over recent years, but every now and then it rears its ugly head, and I have to renew my thinking once again.

What do you have a poverty mindset about?

Money?

Belongings?

Time?

Food?

What do you hide, hoard, and resent people for, when they ask you to share?

What do you hold tighter when God tells you to release some of it? What if today you confessed the stronghold of a poverty mentality in that area? Reject it in the powerful name of Jesus and ask God to help you release it.

Trust that your Good Father has the ability to give you *infinitely more than [you] might ask or think* (Ephesians 3:20), to fully provide so you don't have to freak out and keep the little you have for yourself.

Just open up and release and receive. They're tied together.

Give, and you will receive. Your gift will return to you in full—pressed down, shaken together to make room for more, running over, and poured into your lap. The amount you give will determine the amount you get back. Luke 6:38

37

Evidence of Aidan

———◆———

Every time I look around, I see evidence of Aidan.

His hat (a.k.a. "Hattie" – yes, he named his hat), Kindle, backpack, and necklace are on the kitchen counter. (Out of the fifty outlets in our house, he has to plug his Kindle in on the kitchen counter?)

His toy machine gun and pajama shirt are in the living room.

Two of his schoolbooks are on the floor in the back porch where I'm sitting. His snow boots are in here too.

Two days' worth of clothes and his sleeping bag, pillows, blankets, etc. are on the floor in my bedroom where we let him sleep for the last two nights.

A bowl of Lego pieces is on the table, put there by me as my bare feet find them around the house.

Out the kitchen window, I see a yellow bucket he left in the neighbor's yard.

Every time I look around, I see evidence of Aidan. He doesn't do it on purpose; he's just very active. And if I refrain from being annoyed, I can be glad, because the evidence means one that I love is with me.

Plus, one day he'll be all teenager-y and all he will do is shut his door and mess with his electronics and loud music.

(*At the publishing of this book, Aidan is almost 15, and that is exactly what he does. And also eats food constantly and leaves the dishes in strange places like the floor of his bedroom doorway. And, yes, he gave me permission to publish this. Because he knows he's awesome and I really like him.*)

And one day, before I know it, he won't be here anymore.

***

Every time I look around, I see evidence of Jesus. Unlike Aidan, He does it on purpose, and if I take time to notice, I can be grateful, because He'll always be here, leaving things around so I remember He is with me.

The thunder that woke me up early this morning says spring is finally coming, and the rain washed the snow off my deck.

The sunshine that's flashing in my eyes as I type this says He brings light and warmth.

The cake Terri made and sent along when her son came to spend the night says Jesus even cares about my need for chocolate.

The river opening up has brought the geese and swans back. We refilled the bird feeders, and the singing has begun again. We saw an owl yesterday, and the eagles are hunting. We saw a baby duck paddling along too (clearly he didn't know the eagles were hunting).

A hot shower rarely fails to move me to gratitude. For real, I often thank God for the ability to have a hot shower. (Is that weird? Maybe in another life I lived somewhere with no hot running water.)[1]

***

I want to remind you today not to get so busy looking down at what you are trying to accomplish that you miss looking around and seeing the love Jesus drops all around you.

Before you move on, stop and identify five evidences of Jesus in your past 24 hours. For real, do it. It'll be good for you.

1.

2.

3.

4.

5.

---

[1] No, I do not believe in reincarnation. That was a joke.

38

Wait

———◆———

Last week (around Tuesday or Wednesday) I got some news that was stressful. I gave it to God and decided I wouldn't worry about it or start working on the solution until Monday. I knew it was something I'd need to deal with, but I also knew it was something God would handle for me, so I decided to wait until Monday to even have conversations about it; with myself (in my head), with God, or with the parties involved.

I refused to worry about it until Monday. Every time it popped into my head, I thanked God that He'd already taken care of it, and pushed it right back out of my mind.

Yesterday was Monday. I was still feeling horrible from this cold/flu thing I have, and I thought, *I'm still not going to mess with this today.* Then I got some secondary news that the initial news was slightly incorrect. As in, it's not looking as bad as it did last week.

I am SO GLAD I didn't freak out right away and try to fix the problem or make phone calls or sit down and try to figure it all out. I just waited, and God started shifting the situation for me.

Wait patiently for the Lord. Be brave and courageous. Yes, wait patiently for the Lord. Psalm 27:14

People say *wait on the Lord* kind of a lot.

Oh, just wait on God.

Like it's so easy.

MY WORD IT'S HARD to swallow your instinct to freak out! I think that's why the verse tells us to wait patiently and then it says to *be brave and courageous.*

Breathe. Breathe. Don't freak out. Don't freak out.

Just wait a bit for God to make the answers a little clearer, or to start shifting the situation.

It's hard. Especially when the bill says *due upon receipt.* Or the relational rift looks final. Or you think that person's answer is the end. It LOOKS so bad. But maybe it's not.

Try this: when you're faced with a problem/struggle/bill/diagnosis or stressful news, tell God you're going to establish a "no worries" period of time. 24 hours. Two days. Three days. For a specific period of time, refuse to talk about or worry about your problem. Don't go posting it on Facebook and make a bunch of drama. Tell Him you're not even going to pray about it much, except to keep handing it to Him when you're tempted to mess with it. Simply put it out of your mind and wait.

Every time it pops into your head, thank God that He has taken care of it, and push it back out. If you need to, write your "I'll deal with this then" date and time on your hand. When you worry, look at the date. Is it time yet? No? Then wait.

I mean, God raised Jesus from the dead in three days. What if you asked Him to fix your problem within three days? During those three days, leave it alone. You think Jesus spent those three days fasting and praying and worrying and wondering if God was going to resurrect Him? Nah. He knew the plan. He waited.

If He doesn't fix your problem in your specified no-worries time frame, well, tell Him you'll take whatever action He says at that point. Let's be clear: when it's time to take action, you must do so. Don't confuse "not worrying" with "procrastination".

Be brave and courageous and wait on the Lord. And when it's time to start dealing with it, you might be surprised to find that what you believed to be so bad...isn't.

Yesterday morning Eric received some really discouraging news. I watched his face as I prayed silently, sensing the battle in his heart. To freak out, or not to freak out? Instinctively, I wanted to tell him all the reasons he shouldn't freak out. But this was his test, not mine.

He chose not to freak out. From what I can tell, he didn't let it affect his day. And trust me, I'm really good at knowing if stuff is affecting him.

Late last evening, I received an email that said (essentially) that the news he'd received yesterday morning was blatantly incorrect. Like not even close to right. We actually had good news instead of bad.

He had passed the test. He waited. And God completely reversed the verdict.

I wonder if, had we had freaked out, God would've let the negative news stand. Like if we didn't trust Him anyway, He would just let us work our way through it. Not that He's spiteful, but that if we *choose* to deal with stuff on our own, He will respect our wishes and *let* us.

Instead, I believe He rewarded our un-freak-out-ness and blessed us instead.

Don't freak out! Be brave and courageous. God has something good for you. It's in the plan. Establish a "no-worries" period and wait.

Yet I am confident I will see the LORD's goodness while I am here in the land of the living. Psalm 27:13

39

Homemade Chicken Soup & Stuff

———◆———

Blog Post March 14, 2013

If you are looking for spiritual inspiration, skip this one. Tonight's post is just about what's up this evening. It's for friends I haven't caught up with in a while, people who are bored, and my Mom.

Eric and Braden are south of Chicago tonight, hanging with Brian "Head" Welch from Korn. We met when he came to The Crossing last year, and the connection stuck. We pretty much love that guy, and Eric has made it his goal to make Brian a preacher. The anointing of God is on him in a strong way, so we're excited to see what God does. It'll be rad. (Brian says *rad* a lot. I still don't think I can pull off the regular use of *rad*, but he says I can, and he's the rock star, so.)

Speaking of my Mom, she and Dad live in LA (Lower Alabama), living with and caring for my Grandma until she goes on to Heaven. I'm really proud of my Mom for caring for her mother-in-law for the past four-plus years. Mom told me this morning that she overheard Grandma tell someone the other day, "The food's not too bad here." She gets a little confused and thinks she's in the hospital. She did mention she doesn't care for the eggs. We got a chuckle out of that.

Sometimes you have to chuckle so you don't cry.

I went to Costco with a friend last week and picked up two whole chickens for like $1 per pound. They've been sitting in my fridge since then, so tonight when I walked in the door from work, I bit the bullet and pulled 'em out. I successfully avoided gagging while unwrapping, removing all the nasty stuff from inside their body cavities, rinsing, salting them down, and throwing a few onions into them. I stuck 'em each in an open cake pan, threw them in a 350° oven, and forgot about them.

No, really, I forgot about them. For like two hours. While watching *Wizards of Waverly Place* with Holland & Aidan. When I remembered, ran upstairs and pulled them out, they were perfect. It's actually very easy to roast a chicken. Or a turkey. You newlyweds or newlytryingtocooks, don't be intimidated by cooking whole fowl. Wash/salt/oven. Or just give me a holler when you're fixing to make it and I'll help you out.

Speaking of cooks and me being helpful, a friend asked me the other day about putting a frozen roast in a Crock Pot. Answer: Don't. Yes, it works just fine. People do it all the time. But the slow cooker cooks slowly. Which means it will *slowly* bring your meat to a safe temperature, which means it will linger for quite some time at an unsafe temperature. There.

Thaw your roast overnight in the fridge first. Also don't thaw in warm water. That breeds bacteria. Think of it like a hotel hot tub (icky). If you're in a royal hurry, find something else to cook. Or (sigh) if you *must*, thaw it in the microwave, but that's just unreliable & doesn't thaw evenly.

She asked me how I know that kind of stuff (clearly overlooking my age and 18-year marriage) and I said, "my Mom." Another reason my Mom is awesome. She taught me stuff like that. Or, more accurately, I called her and asked a lot of questions in my first couple years of marriage.

Back to the chickens: A little while later, I spent about twenty minutes de-boning them and now I have a bunch of small containers of chicken in my freezer, ready for whatever I need cooked chicken for.

THEN I took the carcasses (I didn't work too hard to pick them clean; that's just not fun) and threw them in a big pot of water, which is boiling on my stove now, making broth for soup. I'll freeze it. Important: When you do this, boil/simmer for a couple hours or whatever, then strain it. Then put it in the fridge until the fat separates & forms a layer on the top. Overnight is best because it gets really firm. Scrape all that off and you've got a nice, non-fatty broth. Then freeze.

Later, to make soup, just boil[1] and add stuff like chopped onions, garlic, chicken, carrots, and some egg noodles. Salt & pepper to taste. Add chicken bouillon if it's too bland, and then put some Sriracha sauce or cayenne pepper in your bowl if you like spice.

You're thinking, *this is not a cookbook.*

Nope. But it's mine, and I do what I want.

---

[1]Speaking of boiling things, how do you make holy water?
Take regular water and boil the hell out of it.

40

The Garbage Trucks in Maine

◆————

I swear, Maine has the loudest garbage trucks. The biggest problem is that the little streets dead-end at the beach, so there's nowhere for them to turn around. That means the truck driver must back down each street, emitting a loud BEEP BEEP BEEP to warn pedestrians. Then he makes his way back up to the main drag, collecting trash as he goes.

This is what woke me this morning from my lazy vacation sleep-in. That and the very loud birds. (Technically, I think *everything* is too loud in the morning, but we'll set that aside for now.) I thought they were on our street, but later as I sat on my deck drinking myself awake, they showed up right here on Camp Comfort Avenue. BEEP BEEP BEEP, they backed down to the beach end of the road at a surprisingly high speed... then they made their way back up, one guy walking and the other driving, then hopping out to help collect the trash *by hand.*

I quickly switched from wanting to scowl at these men for making so much noise, to feeling sorry for them. The garbage men here have to pick up the big trash cans and dump them by hand into the back of the truck, like in the olden-days. I was so surprised. Maybe in podunk Dirty

South, but on the East Coast? I can't believe it. Don't they know there's a better way?

From my lofty position on my deck – where I sat reading my Bible – I watched these poor, unfortunate souls, living a life they shouldn't have to live. Why? Undoubtedly, the reason they're still functioning that way is financial. Someone has determined that it's not a worthy investment, this idea of offering a better life and an easier job to the local garbage men. I'm guessing they have an inkling that there's a better way to live. Maybe they dream about it at night, riding up high and sidling up to the waiting cans. Pull a lever and the mechanical arm does all the work. (bliss) And then they wake up, and it all floods back. *There's a better way, but no one thinks I'm worth the investment.* I'll bet they'd even pay for the new trucks themselves, if they had the resources. But they don't. Or they wouldn't be doing what they do. It has to start with someone else deciding they're worth it.

For those who haven't caught on, I'm being intentionally melodramatic here about this whole thing. But I saw an analogy and I needed to set it up.

Here's what it made me think:

From our lofty position in our churches – reading our Bibles – so many Christians watch all the poor, unfortunate souls living a life they shouldn't have to live. Why? Undoubtedly, because we've determined that they're not worth our investment. They make too much noise, and they live a life they shouldn't have to, but we think they should figure it out themselves.

"What? I wouldn't be so heartless," you may argue. But do you refuse to help them? Do you refuse to tell them about this better way? Do you refuse to give to the organization that's committed to lifting them up to the life they were created to live?

Remember, there was once a time when you were *that guy.* You were *that girl.* Living a life you shouldn't have to live. And someone thought you were worth the investment — not to just tell you there's a better way — but to financially invest in your life-change. And as you worshiped and learned about the benefits of being in the family of God, you were raised up to a better place. Let's pass along the hope, the joy, the resources we have, so Jesus can do His transforming work in the lives around us.

Also, let's petition this little town to have the garbage trucks start their tour sometime after 10 am so I can sleep a little longer.

41

The Awesomest Non-Christian You Know

———◆———

Have you ever met somebody who is just *awesome*, and thought to yourself, *Too bad she's not a Christian? God created her so naturally cool, I can only imagine the amazing things He'd do with her if she walked into His plan for her life! Clearly He designed her to draw people to herself... and Himself... wow... I really hope she doesn't miss it. She's so funny and has such a big heart to help people; what if she let Him add His "super" to her "natural"?*

World. Changing.

Close your eyes and think for a minute... who is the awesomest non-Christian you know?

What if that person's natural, God-designed awesomeness was enhanced and empowered by His Spirit, direction, and blessing? What kind of incredible life might they live? What influence, joy, favor, and world-bettering might mark that life?

What if YOU were the one who cast that vision to her and invited her to the higher-level life she were created for?

Try it. Tell her you think God made her *above-average!* Tell her to imagine a life with her Creator's favor and blessing. Tell her you know how she can walk into that.

It's easier to tell an addict or struggling person that God can give them a better life than to say the same thing to a have-it-all-together person. You're worried they will reply, "What do I need God for? I have it all." But most people who look like that don't actually feel like they have it all. They struggle with feelings of worthlessness or disappointment when they don't live up to whatever perfectionistic impulses drive them. Behind the scenes, debt may be heavy on their shoulders, or their kids or marriage may be a mess.

Even people who seem already great on the outside need someone to call out the greatness God has placed on their inside. Maybe you're the person for the job. Don't disqualify yourself because your life doesn't look as *together* on the outside. She's thinner, richer, whatever. Don't believe the enemy's lie that you are *less than* whatever ideal you think she lives up to.

You have something *more* that she needs, and don't forget it. So start with a simple compliment, a gift, or some encouragement, and see what happens.

Who's on your mind? Write down their name and be watching for the way God is going to open a door for you to point out their potential when they let Him add His "super" to their "natural".

42

To Ease Discomfort... or Not

———◆———

I was talking with my Mom the other day about moments when someone we're with isn't happy.

The conversation started because one of the grandchildren had decided she didn't like the food we were eating. It made Mom uncomfortable that the child had chosen not to eat.

Uncomfortable situations arise all the time:

You know one of your family members is unhappy.
Your husband isn't having fun at a party and you are.
Something unfortunate happened.
Someone got caught in traffic and missed an important event.
A waiter is rude.
A person is unkind or insensitive, and you/the people you're with have lingering feelings of being unsettled or ill-at-ease.

What do you do?

Naturally, our instinct (especially as women/mothers/pleasers) is to try to ease the discomfort of the situation. We offer multiple other food options, make suggestion after suggestion of how to make the person comfortable (often to no avail), or offer the ever-annoying *let's look on the bright side* encouragements.

As I talked with Mom, here's what came to mind: Don't. Don't try to ease the discomfort.

I said, "Mom, sometimes we feel bad that someone is uncomfortable, so we try and try and try to make them feel better, usually with things we think would make US feel better, were we in their situation." So the grandchild had chosen to not eat. It was the child's choice, yet Mom felt bad about it.

I reminded her, "Mom, it was *her choice*. You don't need to try to make her feel better about her choice." Your personal solution to what you perceive to be her problem probably won't help her anyway.

Sometimes the situation is *not* the result of the person's choices; it is an accident, or it's the doing of another person that makes us/them uncomfortable. And our instinct is to tell all those involved, "It's OK! It'll work out. Let's feel better about this. Put yourself in *their* shoes. It's not as bad as it seems..." Blah, blah, blah... all to try to make ourselves feel better about what was just a crappy, unfortunate situation.

Sometimes we just need to *feel* the unfortunate moment.

Blithely wiping away and glossing over every little situation makes for shallow character.

Feeling, dealing with, and coming out the other side of uncomfortable situations grows maturity. Let your children feel uncomfortable sometimes.

Don't force people to be *your version of happy*. If he says he's fine, and you should go enjoy the party for a few more minutes, go ahead. Don't try to make him seem happier about where he is. Let him *be*.

If there's nothing you can do about someone else's choice, just chalk it up to humanity being flawed, and turn it around to gratitude that Jesus gives us a rich life despite the actions of others. Tell Him thanks for the good stuff. But don't try to make it better than it was. It just *was.*

Be thankful in all circumstances, for this is God's will for you who belong to Christ Jesus. 1 Thessalonians 5:18

> *Don't worry about anything; instead, pray about everything. Tell God what you need, and thank him for all he has done. Then you will experience God's peace, which exceeds anything we can understand. His peace will guard your hearts and minds as you live in Christ Jesus. Philippians 4:6-7*

Relax. The darker moments are part of the weaving that make the fabric of a colorful life.

43

When Jesus Played Possum

———◆———

Then Jesus got into the boat and started across the lake with His disciples. Suddenly, a fierce storm struck the lake, with waves breaking into the boat. But Jesus was sleeping. Matthew 8:23-24

Hang on a minute.

They got into the boat and started across the lake. SUDDENLY a storm hit, but Jesus was (already) sleeping? Really.

Has it ever occurred to anyone that He might have been faking? Playing possum? Feigning fatigue? Intensely examining the backs of His eyelids?

Mark's account of the story says this. *But <u>soon</u> a fierce storm came up. High waves were breaking into the boat, and it began to fill with water. Jesus was sleeping... Mark 4:37-38, emphasis mine*

I suppose I'm not the first person to think this, but it was a first for me when I read it this week. He was in a fishing boat, not a yacht. He was probably lying on some planks with His head on a balled-up robe. Not exactly easy to fall asleep fast, nor stay asleep with waves splashing in.

Jesus had a point to make, and I'm thinking that He was chilling out, waiting for the storm, so He could sit up and show off... and reveal the hearts of His disciples.

I like Mark's version, so we'll continue with it.

The disciples woke him up, shouting, "Teacher, don't you care that we're going to drown?" Mark 4:38

Interesting. Mark said they called Him "Teacher."

Makes me think of Indiana Jones...He's a professor with a whole bunch of adventure/survival skills.

"Holy moly, Professor, we've got a storm! Don't you care that we're going to drown?!"

I don't think they really thought He could do anything except provide an extra set of hands for rowing. Because they simply saw Him as their teacher.

He woke, silenced the storm. *Then he asked them, "Why are you afraid? Do you still have so little faith?" Mark 4:40*

Still. After hearing My messages and seeing Me do miracles, do you *still* think I'm just a teacher?

Apparently so.

The disciples were absolutely terrified. "Who is this man?" They asked each other. "Even the wind and waves obey Him!" Mark 4:41

Who is this *man*?

Teacher. Man. What they said about Jesus revealed what they believed about Him.

***

What do you believe about Jesus?

Your words reveal what you believe.

What do you say?

Is He just a good teacher with some nice fortune-cookie help for life?

Do you largely ignore Him?

Do you talk about Him? Or do you just talk about church?

Do you refer to Him as a good man, or do you call upon the power of His name to conquer your struggles and calm your storms?

What you say about Jesus reveals Who you believe He is, and what you believe He can do for you.

Do you want to follow a nice teacher?

Or do you want to be *just a little terrified* by the power that rides in the boat with you?

Do you want to get through life with an extra set of hands, like a crutch you can lean on as you limp?

Or do you want to reign in life in the company of the Creator of the universe, Whose voice spoke the world into existence and will speak your storms into silence?

It's your call. And it completely depends on what you believe about Jesus.

He might lay low at times to bring you to a place where you are forced to reveal what you really believe about Him and His power in your life, but don't freak out. He's probably just playing possum, hoping you'll ask Him to sit up and show off.

44

Then Look Up

———◆———

Me, putting chili in the Crock Pot: "I get dizzy when I look down."

Braden, making instant oatmeal: "Then look up."

***

My back has been "busted" since Friday. In the family of pastors, everything crappy happens on Fridays or Saturdays. Satan is suuuuper predictable. Jack stuff up before the weekend, which is when we have the greatest opportunity to advance the Kingdom of Jesus Christ.

Technically I started the process Wednesday night when I went for a run with Tracy. I was so pleased with myself - 2.4 miles in about 35 minutes. Yes, I'm slow. But I'm getting exercise and not hating it. So there. Thursday at our St. Cloud campus, I felt my back tightening. Friday morning I was praying I'd get through my speech at the Aflac state convention thing. (Hey, when God gives us an opportunity for influence, we take it, right?) By the time I got home, I could hardly get out of my car and into the house. It's my psoas (hip-flexor) muscle, for those who know about that stuff. I learned all about it last fall.

So I've been binge watching Hulu, icing, stretching, praying, believing, crying as my legs give out when I attempt to walk, trying really hard to think positive thoughts, and lying in my bed feeling helpless and worthless while everybody else gets to go change the world. This weekend, our church had its biggest attendance in months, lots of people gave their lives to Jesus, and I sat in my bathtub turning into a wrinkled old prune.

My heart was a little wrinkled, too.

Why does this happen to me?

Is God trying to tell me something? Don't exercise? (ha) Slow down? Quit my job and watch Hulu?

My sweet friend Britney said, "Just think! God is doing a work in you! Just sit with Him, and you'll look back later and see what He was doing." And she reminded me of another time in my life that I was out of commission for a while – and He really *did* do some cool things in me.

But I don't feel like sitting with Him.

Technically, I'm not even *supposed* to sit. Walk around or lie down: those are my options. I'm actually typing this while lying down. It's annoying. Blessedly, I'm way better today. A chiropractic adjustment and brutal massage yesterday helped. (I say *brutal* to eradicate images of an indulgent spa massage – it was more like Lamaze-style breathing while someone dug into my abdomen to reach that *&@% psoas muscle.)

This morning, I can walk. But I woke up with mild vertigo.

Are you *freaking kidding me?*

I get dizzy when I look down.

I. get. dizzy. when. I. look. down.

When I look down, around me, at pain, problems, roadblocks, stressors, if/then scenarios, people, schedules, unknowns... I get a little dizzy. The world spins and things don't make sense. And the more I try to get it all straight in my mind, the more confusing it all becomes, and the more helpless I feel.

So I look up.

No, I can't actually see God peering at me from the clouds, but I can see Him with eyes of faith.

I imagine Him seeing my situation from His perspective and not being stressed at all. I think about His heart for me—how much He loves me. I don't know what He is working out for me, but I remember what He's done in the past, and I believe He's the same today as He was yesterday. This allows me to trust Him.

I ask Him for a glimpse of His grace in this difficult place.

When you're looking for grace, you find it.

Look up today.

Don't look down. It'll make you dizzy.

Look up.

45

If You Are Crabby

———◆———

Take a nap.

The Lord is my Shepherd, I shall not want. He <u>makes me lie down</u> in green pastures. Psalm 23:2 (NIV)

Don't be that cranky toddler who refuses to take a nap and makes everyone else suffer for it.

The end.

46
Too Busy to Feel the Burn

---◆---

I have a passion for keeping a Sabbath rest: one day each week in which we do not work. It is set apart in Scripture (it's in one of the Ten Commandments!) as a holy portion of time in which we connect with God. We rest and relax and get out of the crazy and remember to be grateful and to nurture our relationships with God and each other.

It's the only way I believe we accomplish everything we need to without going insane: Give God His day and let Him bless the work we do on the rest of the days, enabling us to get it all done!

A million reasons exist why people have a hard time taking a rest, not the least of which is straight-up *fear we won't get crap done.* But last night I was reminded of another reason I believe people actually avoid taking a (real) rest from the busyness of life. Here's what happened:

I was pulling rolls out of the oven and bumped my right hand on the oven rack, burning the knuckle on my thumb. It hurt.

But I was busy getting dinner on the table, and I quickly forgot about it. We had dinner, sat around the table for a while answering questions from our conversation card box, and then I retreated to my room with a chocolate truffle and a glass of wine to relax while the family cleaned up the kitchen (it's our deal: I cook; they clean). I decided to take a bath, which is one of my favorite ways to force myself to sit and relax.

The hot water that felt so blessedly wonderful on my tired muscles hit that spot on my thumb and reminded me, *Oh yeah! I have a burn!* Ouch! It wasn't until I detached from the busyness and paid attention to myself and my well-being that I was able to (actually, forced to) face the fact that I got burned earlier.

Why do we have such a hard time just being *still*? I believe partly because it's hard to face the fact that we hurt. Or are unhappy. Or got burned yesterday. It's easier to keep moving and keep the TV on or the music playing or the games going so we don't have the space to feel the burn.

Activity is so good at numbing pain. Choosing to tune out the noise of the world and settle in with just you, yourself, and God brings that pain to the surface.

So maybe you tend to do one of two things:

a) Refuse to rest. Stay so busy in life that you don't have time to acknowledge that you've been burned or that you're falling apart inside.

or

b) Choose to chill but turn to various other numbing activities... so you can "relax" but not be forced to feel the pain. Too much drink, food, entertainment, gossip, porn, unhealthy indulgences... they provide the illusion of rest/relaxation without feeling the burn that happened yesterday, last week, or seven years ago.

This is why true rest – the rest that God offers – includes an honest assessment of where we are. An acknowledgement of the pain, but then an intentional handing of the situation to Jesus. It requires letting

160

go of our burdens and letting Him handle them. It is a choice to obey His directive: *Be still and know that I am God. Psalm 46:10*

Give all your worries and cares to God, for He cares about you. 1 Peter 5:7

Dump them on Him, tell Him the pain. Cough it up. He knows it's there anyway, and He's not afraid. We're the ones who are so reluctant to be honest about it. But then the second part of that verse says, *for He cares for you.* After you give Him the pain, let Him care for you and speak soothing words over your soul. Ask Him to help you know He's with you and that He cares.

Don't get too busy to feel the burn, because eventually those wounds scab and scar and dull your ability to be real and authentic. Cover-ups become a way of life.

Take the time and space to do a body-check. Locate the splinters and uncomfortable things, acknowledge that they hurt, and then hand them to Jesus. Release the people who hurt you. Receive the healing power of the Spirit of God.

Enter into a time of true, healthy rest and let Him refresh your soul. And then return to life from a place of wholeness.

47

How Not to Worry About Money

———————◆———————

How many of you moms want your children to wake up every morning and think, *I wonder how I will get food today?* No! You want them to wake up and *know* they will be cared for and fed because they are in constant connection with you and what you provide for them.

God is a good Father who wants His kids to live in full confidence that all the resources that we need for survival will be provided by Him. He doesn't want us to stress out and think that it's all up to us! He wants us to be in constant connection with Him and what He provides for us. In fact, Jesus repeatedly tells us not to worry:

> *...I tell you not to worry about everyday life—whether you have enough food and drink, or enough clothes to wear. Isn't life more than food, and your body more than clothing? Look at the birds. They don't plant or harvest or store food in barns, for your heavenly Father feeds them. And aren't you far more valuable to him than they are? Can all your worries add a single moment to your life? And why worry about your clothing? Look at the lilies of the field and how they grow. They don't work or make their clothing, yet Solomon in all his glory was not dressed as beautifully as they are. And if God cares so wonderfully for wildflowers that are here today and thrown into the*

fire tomorrow, he will certainly care for you. Why do you have so little faith?

So don't worry about these things, saying, 'What will we eat? What will we drink? What will we wear?' These things dominate the thoughts of unbelievers, but your heavenly Father already knows all your needs. Seek the Kingdom of God above all else, and live righteously, and he will give you everything you need. Matthew 6:25-33

You're probably thinking, *OK, great. But don't worry is waaaaaay easier said than done. HOW do I not worry?*

I'm glad you asked. I'll tell you what works for me. This is how I don't worry. It's not a mind game or self-control or a mantra to repeat. It's truth found in the Bible. And living by Bible truth always brings me inner peace.

Here we go:

Like the Sabbath is *time* set apart as holy and helps us to connect with God, Scripture says there is *money* that is set apart as holy and helps us to connect with God.

The money that is set apart as holy to connect with God is called the *tithe*. *Tithe* is a math term that means *tenth*. As a fraction, it's 1/10. As a percentage, it's 10%.

The concept demonstrated throughout Scripture and millennia by God-followers is this: we return to God the first tenth of our income from Him – it is His holy (set apart) portion – and He blesses the part that remains in our hands.

> *"Bring all the tithes into the storehouse so there will be enough food in my Temple. If you do," says the Lord of Heaven's Armies, "I will open the windows of heaven for you. I will pour out a blessing so great you won't have enough room to take it in! Try it! Put me to the test! Your*

crops will be abundant, for I will guard them from insects and disease. Your grapes will not fall from the vine before they are ripe," says the Lord of Heaven's Armies.
Malachi 3:10-11

These verses tell us that the heart of God is to bless you financially. He says to bring His part into His house so that the ministry of spreading the Good News can continue. And then He says He will pour out provision on you. Not only will He pour out new blessings, but the description He gives includes protecting the assets you already own.

In other words, give God His part, and He will bless your part.

Eric and I have been living by this concept for more than twenty years. We always return the first 10% of all we receive through paychecks or gifts or unexpected income, straight to God at His house (the church).

We don't wait until the end of the month to see what we have left. We start with God and connect our money supply to Him immediately by opening our hands, giving Him His part, and saying, *You're in this with us.*

And this is why I do not worry about money, no matter how big the bills are or how much uncertainty lies ahead. It's not my problem. The unlimited resources of the Kingdom of Heaven belong to my Dad, and He always provides when I stay connected to Him by doing finances His way.

48

Innocent?

———◆———

Hi.

After reading in Titus this morning and scribbling frantically in my journal, I decided to share this with you.

Everything is pure to those whose hearts are pure. But nothing is pure to those who are corrupt and unbelieving, because their minds and consciences are corrupted. Titus 1:15

Break it down:

Everything is pure to those whose hearts are pure.

Innocent people do not live a lifestyle of being suspicious of others.

But nothing is pure to those who are corrupt and unbelieving, because their minds and consciences are corrupted.

I'm not thinking "corrupt and unbelieving" means horrible people; I'm thinking it's referring to those who simply lack faith to believe God's truth (which is any of us on any given day, right?).

When you carry guilt and have allowed the enemy a foothold in some area of your life, your *mind and conscience* are corrupt. Your thinking gets a little skewed because you *believe* you're not innocent. And the lies about yourself and others creep in:

Everybody and everything becomes suspicious.

You question people's choices and motives.

You envy others' successes.

You look for hidden meaning in a look, a statement, a text, a post, a photo.

You think others are judging you, *because you are judging yourself.*

You indulge in the drama of other people so you can forget your own.

Been there?

Ever catch yourself getting cynical, suspicious? Pointing out other people's...*whatever*?

Yeah, I've been there.

BUT...

If you're guilt-free, forgiven, and loved...

If you're declared innocent by Jesus...

If you believe that He has given you His righteousness by His work on the cross...

You can extend the same grace to others.

You can assume they're innocent, because God assumes you are.

You can believe the best about others because God believes the best about *you*...

...and *you believe Him.*

Love believes the best. 1 Corinthians 13:7 (ISV)

I have no reason to look for wrong in the lives of others. I trust that God can correct them if they're wrong, just like He does for me.

Perfect love casts out fear. 1 John 4:18

I have no fear that somehow someone else's joy means there won't be enough for me. I believe I'm safe in God's love for me.

Other people won't bother you nearly as much if your heart is innocent, believing God's love and grace is poured on you.

This is kinda freeing, isn't it?

Today I'm going to start by letting God declare me innocent. I'll line up with His heart for my day, my work, my choices, my world. I'll choose to believe His love. And I'll extend the same to others.

Will you?

49

Stuck

———————◆———————

I've spent the last 32 hours just off an exit in rural northern Iowa.

In a hotel, but not the awesome kind.

I'm stuck.

Technically, I could have left today, but I've become a diligent student of the Minnesota road conditions website, and the state patrol and everyone important has been saying that we shouldn't travel if we don't have to.

And the only "have to" in my near future is to be at the grand opening of my church's new building tomorrow night.

So Aidan and I are hanging out watching *Full House*. Steve Urkel is guest starring.

I've worked on my *People Mover* book a bit today. About a week ago I told Eric I'd like to get away for a couple of days and stay at a (very nice) hotel and work on my book, undisturbed.

Instead I got a (not nice) hotel with my 11-year-old son watching

SpongeBob. I should have been more specific about my request.

How'd I get here? And why am I stuck?

I had needed to attend a meeting in downtown Des Moines at 9 am yesterday, so Aidan and I drove down Wednesday evening and spent the night with Eric's parents. We started to get on the highway at 11 am yesterday just as hail began. We did a U-turn and cowered under a gas station overhang and then started again. Rain turned to snow, and by the time we hit Mason City (three hours later), I was getting a little nervous. When I started fishtailing right beside a snowplow, I decided to call a time-out.

Over tacos and cinnamon twists, Aidan and I decided to stop for the night.

Today was sunny; deceptively pleasant. But I-35 was shut down in northern Iowa and southern Minnesota. Last I checked, the southbound lanes were still closed around Albert Lea. I'm going north, but, really, those lanes are only a few yards apart.

So. When you're stuck, what do you do?

Look around, see what you *can* do, and do that, apparently.

1. I did something good for myself. Fortunately I had my gym clothes in my trunk, so I went down to the fitness room and ran my VERY FIRST 5K! 3.1 miles in 36 minutes. For me, that's awesome. And I'm pretty proud of myself.

2. I did something good for my family (sort of). I chopped the ice off my car, shoveled the drift behind it, and Aidan and I headed carefully to Dollar General, where we blew $100 on lamps (needed) and groceries (don't judge; I'm well aware there are no healthy foods available there). I feel like I never have time to get groceries at home, so why not do it today while we're stuck?

When we returned and confirmed the road conditions, we decided to stay another night. So we caught the end of *Ice Age* (so apropos) and then walked downstairs to Bennigan's, where I let Aidan have cheesecake for supper. I figured, what the heck. It's not often we're stuck.

When you're stuck, sometimes, you might think stuff like this:

How did I get here?

Whose fault is it?

How could I have avoided this?

If you're a Jesus-follower, you probably add things like this:

What is God trying to teach me?

What's He up to?

How's He going to work this out for good?

I've thought through this a bit. I don't even feel like my meeting in Des Moines was profitable. I would have been more helpful staying home and helping Eric host a group of pastors we had visiting on Thursday. So, to make myself feel better about being stuck, I keep trying to invent ways God might use this situation. I try to make myself feel better by saying how good it has been to rest before a huge weekend at church (plus we have houseguests coming). Maybe Aidan just needed time with his mom. Maybe the other two kiddos needed time with Daddy. Maybe I made a connection in Des Moines that will prove beneficial in the future. Who knows? Only God.

Do you do this too? Try to figure out how to justify whatever's happening? You think, *If I could just step back and get the whole picture, if I could solve the why-did-this-happen puzzle, I could feel better about all this.*

I guess that the simple lesson here is that when we're stuck, the best thing to do is look around and see what you *can* do, and do what you can. Beyond that, just trust that God's working on something behind the scenes. I may never know why this trip happened like it did, but God doesn't waste time or situations.

And we know that God causes everything to work together for the good of those who love God and are called according to his purpose for them. Romans 8:28

So it's all good. The situation is not great. But it's good. Because God is good.

I'm just hoping the electricity doesn't go out in our hotel tonight. Last night, that just wasn't cool.

50

Doing Hard Things

———◆———

Blog Post December 9, 2013

If you were at church on Sunday, you know my voice deteriorated quickly. I was actually pretty sick. Praise God that in our times of weakness, He steps in and makes us strong! Of all my preaching times, this was probably the most mentally challenging – shoving out the mind monsters that tried to tell me I wouldn't be able to get through five services. I was so excited to share, and Eric said he'd come and finish Sunday for me if he needed to, but we both knew God had given ME the word for this weekend. I confidently asked for and declared healing in Jesus' name, but for some reason, God allowed me to "play hurt". So I confidently declared that I had His power in me to do the work. I didn't freak out or get victim-y, because what would that accomplish?

In this moment, I'm sitting in my bed, typing and coughing, surrounded by Kleenex. I spent today working via phone, email, and FaceTime. It ain't pretty. But I'm supremely grateful that He carried me through the weekend. And having survived that, I'll be more confident the next time He calls me to pull on my big-girl pants and do something hard.

I don't know what you're up against this week. If you think about all of the stuff you need to accomplish, you might get a little bit sick to your stomach. If you think about how hard it will be, or whether or not you'll physically be able to accomplish it, you'll start to freak out.

Think about what you're thinking about! Just focus on your Father's loving heart and His strength to help you accomplish what you need to DESPITE His apparent unwillingness to remove your obstacle! He's building your faith and your courage! Stay in faith and let Him carry you forward. When you're on the other side of this busy season, you want to look back and be proud of how well you trusted – and not annoyed with yourself for freaking out.

For I can do everything through Christ, who gives me strength. Philippians 4:13

51

Are You Feelin' It?

———◆———

I can feel love for you without it affecting you at all.

Think about this.

I can feel – inside my heart and emotions – love FOR you.

But it will not affect you unless I figure out how to cause YOU to feel my love.

How would I do this?

I would have to act.

I would need to take some sort of action to transfer this force within me to you, in a way that you would recognize as my love.

This would work best if I knew what your "love language" is. Do you feel love through words? Maybe I could look into your eyes and talk about how I feel about you and what delights me about you.

Do you feel love through actions? I could wash your dishes or take care of some tasks that have you overwhelmed right now.

Do you feel love through companionship? I could sit by you in a coffee shop and not talk all that much. Just *be* with you.

Do you feel love through physical contact? I could pat you on the shoulder when I walk by or give you a hug when I see you.

Love is not complete until it's transferred from one heart to another in a way that is felt and understood by both.

***

...You delight in showing unfailing love. Micah 7:18

You will show us your faithfulness and unfailing love. Micah 7:20

I've always known that God loves me. My parents taught me well. I mean, come on, Jesus must have loved me a lot to give His life for me.

God showed His love for us in this: while we were still sinners, Christ died for us. Romans 5:8

I know in my head that He loves me. The Bible says so. History says so. But according to those verses in Micah, God gets *delight* out of *showing* me His love. Verse 15 says, *I will do mighty miracles for you.*

That means He *does stuff* to *show* us His love, and because He's our Creator, He *knows our love languages.*

Maybe this is obvious to you, but today I was reminded that He really likes showing *me* His love! And in His perfect understanding of me, He can speak *my* language!

I betcha five bucks He speaks yours too.

Why don't you ask Him today, right this minute, to show you His love? So you don't have to imagine it or decide it or look at history to see it. You can see it today. He'd probably get a great kick out of speaking your language and making you feel how He feels about you.

52

Go For the Ask

———————◆———————

I found this little bit of awesomeness in my time with God this morning and thought maybe it will help you too.

If any of you lacks wisdom, you should ask God, who gives generously to all without finding fault, and it will be given to you. James 1:5

If you need wisdom, ask God, and it will be given to you. But here's the part I really love. *Without finding fault.* Meaning, if you find yourself in a tough spot and ask God for wisdom, He will NOT look back at you and list all the reasons why it's your own dumb fault for getting into that spot. He will NOT make sure you feel sufficiently guilty before He gives you the ability to make a good decision.

I can't even tell you how many times I've missed what God had to offer because I assumed it was my own fault that I was where I was, so I figured I had to get myself back out. So I didn't even ask!

But this Scripture says He simply *gives generously to all*.

It doesn't even cost you. Jesus paid for your free access to God's wisdom.

He grants a treasure of common sense to the honest. Proverbs 2:7

What do you need some wisdom for today? A problem that has been nagging at you for six months? A dilemma that just came up? Get honest about where you are today and ask God for the brains to get you through or out of or around your situation. This says your request will be granted.

And He's not stingy about it. He doesn't eke out a tiny little smidge of smarts.

He grants *a treasure of common sense.* A *treasure*, not a *tip*! An abundant wealth of all you need to make the choices that will carry you someplace good.

Go for the ask. Ask God to help you know the wise thing to do in your situation. This might be obvious, but go ahead and make plans to obey what He says. It's super annoying when someone asks for your help and then rejects it, right? So don't do that to God when He's being all generous with His infinite wisdom.

Roll with what He gives you, and see what happens.

For real. Stop right now and ask.

Do it.

Did you?

OK, now keep your eyes open for His answer that can come in the form of faith-filled friends, portions of Scripture, circumstances, and an instinct in your heart that lines up with what is true and right and *wise.*

53

Think for Yourself

———◆———

People are easily influenced. Heck, *I'm* easily influenced. If my friend Tracy says my outfit's OK, I take her word for it and literally don't give it another thought. Because she's cool. If Chrissie says a song is awesome, and I should listen to it, a-Googling I will go. If the commercial says that I can eat the brownie and actually burn calories by chewing it, I'm very likely to believe it and go buy the brownie. (Well, maybe not, but...)

Not only are we *easily influenced*, but we also want *to influence* others. I was talking with a woman once who INSISTED that her way of doing such-and-such was absolutely, completely, finally, THE ONLY way to do it. And she believed in it so much that she bought me all the supplies and hand-wrote out all the instructions. She wanted to influence me.

Along the same lines, I personally take a health supplement that I absolutely, completely believe has prevented illness for me for at least a year. So I influence others to buy it. Or I give them some of mine. I try to influence others to eat the food I like, to send their kids to my kids' school, to shop where I shop, to like country music. Sometimes this is a conscious thing: "Kelsey, you have GOT to like ketchup." Other times, it's unconscious: "I shop at Plato's Closet; it's got cool clothes that are way cheaper than retail. Check there for a Twirl dress..."

I think that it's part of human nature to want others to experience the same thing as you. We are wired with a desire to have something in common with the next person. "You have a 8-year-old boy? My son is 9!" (All excited, like, "Yay! We're practically sisters!")

And if the person disagrees or doesn't make the connection, we feel kind of weird. Gina says, "Oh, don't eat at _____. Their food tastes like crap..." And Emily responds, "Really? Oh, wow, I love that place; it's my absolute favorite." [Insert awkward pause here.] It's more likely that Emily will just nod and smile to avoid making Gina feel judged or disagreed-with.

Even more concerning (or annoying) is someone who tries to influence others based upon something she hasn't experienced herself. Consider Jess, who says, "Don't use _____'s products. They're crap. They fall apart after like two uses." Mary replies, "Really? Did that happen to you?" Jess: "Well, no, actually I've never used it, but Bob's brother Don said that happened with his food chopper." So here's Jess campaigning against a product she's never used, based on gossip about someone else's experience.

*It is not good to have **zeal without knowledge,** nor to be hasty and miss the way.* Proverbs 19:2

When Braden was a toddler, I coached cheerleading. Our team was green. So we were always yelling, "GO GREEN!" Well, Braden LOVED to yell, "GO BLUE!" with great zeal. He was too young to know why we were yelling GREEN and the other team was yelling BLUE, so he picked the color that looked good to him, regardless of the meaning behind the color. He had *zeal without knowledge,* and without knowing it, he was campaigning for the wrong team.

I guess my point boils down to this: Do your homework. Taste the food. Listen to the music. Try the product. But, above all, experience it for yourself before opening your mouth about it. Don't believe everything you read; everyone else's opinion; everyone else's perspective. This might surprise you, but *people lie.* Sometimes intentionally, and sometimes not. People have issues, and they project them onto others. Steer clear of being the fool who gets sucked into someone else's crazy. Don't accidentally campaign for the wrong thing.

You don't have to like the restaurant. You don't have to wear the clothes. You don't have to send your kids to the school. You don't have to go to the church. You don't have to like the candidate or the celebrity. But make your decision based on your own experience of the actual place, person, or product, and don't campaign *for or against* something unless you've done your homework and experienced it for yourself.

God has created a vast variety of people with different styles, tastes, preferences, needs, and ways of connecting with Him.

The world has created a vast variety of people with different sorts of baggage, experiences, hurts, habits, hang-ups, defenses, needs, sensitivities, and expectations.

Don't go yelling, "GO BLUE!", and get other people to yell it, too, when you have no idea what it means. Figure it out for yourself.

54
The Bar and Hurting People

◆————

Much of my life is spent within the walls of The Crossing Church. It's where I'm called to be, to play my role in the body of Christ. Working in a church provides a form of insulation. I am often insulated from a world of people whose hurts/dysfunctions/needs I only see when they walk through our doors. Or when I watch the news or hear about someone's "story" – which is often immediately followed by the life-change-happy-ending.

I wrote this on my blog a few years ago, and it reminded me why we continue to reach out and share the hope of Jesus. I hope you'll catch this vision, too. Part of the freedom to twirl includes opening our arms to those who need the same hope we have found.

***

About once a year I go out with a few girlfriends to karaoke. I love to sing, but I'm not a soloist. As we got ready to go last night, I told my friend, "I just realized I'm going to sing karaoke in a bar in a small town where my face is on a billboard." Not because I was worried about my reputation, but because I'm not that great of a singer.

The upside is that many of the people would be drunk and wouldn't judge me.

The downside is that many of the people were drunk.

[Two places people aren't judged quite so much as the normal world: the bar, and church. Or at least one *should* be the church.]

I'm really tired this morning. Despite my fancy new sleep mask, I woke up as Braden was leaving for school. Right away today – well, even last night as we drove home – I have been filled with compassion for the people I saw and talked with last night.

There were a few uncomfortable moments and awkward conversations: "I really wish you wouldn't ask for an offering at church. That turns people off. You need to consider that." And, "I went to Crossing Recovery tonight, and now I'm drinking, but I'm sure God will forgive me tomorrow."

But there were also a few moments when I knew I was exactly where I was supposed to be. I met two girls who say they'll be coming to church with our mutual friend. I got to give a huge hug to a girl who recently met Jesus at The Crossing. I got to hear a Crossing guy sing, and told him with a voice like that, he *needs* to be singing at church. (He replied that he only sings with a few beers in him, so we'll have to work on that...)

And I met a former Crossing volunteer who was feeling guilty for where she was and what she was doing.

I tried to encourage her. *Jesus loves you. You're OK.*

She looked back at me. *I'm not OK.*

I prayed with her before we left. She was very drunk, but this morning I'm praying that she remembers what I said, and that God's Spirit will let that encounter be a starting place for a return home to Him.

I'm not saying you need to go to a bar to get a refresher on God's heart for hurting people. If you struggle with alcoholism or sin associated with the bar environment, *run, Forrest, run!*

I am saying that I'm glad I went. Not because I had a fun time with a few friends and killed "Black Horse and a Cherry Tree."

But because I realized that *those people* – the ones who are looking for hope and life at the bottom of a tall Mich Golden Light – they're the ones I've been called to love. And not just hypothetically. And not just when they come into my church.

They are everywhere.

They are our neighbors and the grocery clerk and insurance agent and school teacher.

And they need Jesus.

Some of us might need to go to the bar more often.

55

Lotion and Battery Chargers and Delayed Dreams

———◆———

Me: "Can you put some lotion on my back?" (Squirting some lotion onto his hand.)

Eric: "This hand is dirty. Hang on." (Switching the little blob from left to right.)

Me: "What."

Him: "I just coiled the extension cord in the garage. I forgot to wash my hands."

Me: (Gross, but) "Oh! Did your battery charge?"

Him: "Yes."

Me: "How much?"

Him: (Sheepishly) "Full charge."

Me: "REALLY."

Flashback to last night

He returns from the garage, "It's still not charged. Maybe the wall outlet doesn't work right."

(Two hours earlier)

Coming in the door, "I must have ruined my battery by unplugging it for awhile before it was fully charged earlier. Sometimes if you mess with the charge, it ruins the battery. It's only 2% more charged than it was earlier."

(Before that)

"I *just bought* that battery charger after my other one was stolen. Maybe it just doesn't work. Maybe I need to return it."

(Before that)

"Oh man, my battery's only at 67%, and it's been two hours."

(Yesterday morning)

"I think I'll go fishing, but I need to charge my trolling motor battery."

Back to today

Me: "This is SUCH an analogy for your life!"

Him: "I suppose so."

Me: "You should write about this!"

Him: "YOU write about this."

Me: "Fine. I will."

Why this struck me

You wake up one morning (or one month or year) and have an idea. "I would like to _____." And you think about how fun/cool/exciting/effective/wonderful/nice it would be.

So you start with your steps of preparation to make it happen. Enroll in a class/set up a plan/submit an application/buy something/sell something/talk to someone/plug something in.

And then you wait.

And you check back every few hours/days/months/years.

The progress is slow.

So. Slow.

So you start looking around at all the moving parts and begin questioning things.

This isn't happening how it's supposed to.
This isn't working right.
Maybe I'm using the wrong equipment.

You question yourself.

What if I'm not qualified for this?
What if I'm doing this wrong?
Maybe I broke something along the way.

The blaming starts.

If she hadn't said that...
If he had only done...
I'll bet it's his/her/their/my/our/God's fault this isn't working.

And finally you give up the stressing and just decide to go to bed/rest/wait it out/have an *oh, screw it all/give it to God* moment.

And one morning you wake up and realize IT happened.

Even though Eric was convinced that his battery was not going to fully charge... Even though he eventually decided (because he's a really good man) to take me grocery shopping instead of fishing yesterday, he left that thing plugged in. And the battery charged. Today, he can go fishing if he wants to.

My word for you (and me and Eric – all of us) today is this: It may not look like anything is happening.

The progress may seem SO. SLOW.

But STAY PLUGGED IN.

Because the dreams and ideas God has put in your heart are *still in His heart for you.*

Don't give up. Maybe stop stressing. Stop blaming. Choose to rest. But don't unplug.

At the right time, you'll be fully charged, and you'll see it – whatever IT is for you – come to pass.

"For I know the plans I have for you," declares the Lord, "plans to prosper you and not to harm you, plans to give you hope and a future." Jeremiah 29:11 (NIV)

56

Prepositions

———◆———

The year was 1983. Miss Parker's 4th grade class at Dale County Christian School in Ozark, Alabama, stood dutifully to the left of our desks, reciting in unison the list of prepositions.

Aboard

About

Above

Across

After

Against

Along

Among

Around

At

Before

Behind

Below

Beneath

Beside

Between

Beyond

But

By

Down

During

Except

For

From

In

Inside

Into

Like

Near

Off

Of

On

Over

Past

Since

Through

Throughout

To

Toward

Under

Underneath

Until

Up

Upon

WITH

WITHIN

WITHOUT![1]

(We always yelled the last three. I think because we were glad we were done.)

***

The year is 2016. I woke up before the sun and lay in my bed with a song stuck in my head. *I believe my God is good.* Over and over, the song played. And I thought about how good God is. And what a difference that makes in how I feel about my life.

If I believe that God doesn't just *do* good sometimes, but that He *is* goodness itself.

He *is* good.

I was thinking God is good *to* me.

He is good *for* me. He's good on my behalf!

He is good *around* me. *Surely, LORD, you bless the righteous; you surround them with your favor as with a shield. Psalm 5:12 (NIV)*

He is good *during* hard times, conversations, and situations.

He is good *toward* others! And that doesn't lesson His goodness *toward* me! There's not a shortage of God's favor. Ever.

He is good *with* me. We get to do good together.

He is good *within* me. He brings me crazy peace that doesn't make sense! (Philippians 4:7)

He is good *without* fail. God is never bad at being good.

Do not be afraid or discouraged, for the LORD will personally go ahead of you. He will be with you; he will neither fail you nor abandon you. Deuteronomy 31:8

I was like, wow, there's a lot of prepositions involving the goodness of God.

And that's how I came to be reciting the prepositions in my bed at 6:00 this morning.

There's a preposition in the (complete) list that wasn't included in the one I memorized. It's the word *despite.*

God is good. Despite me.

Despite: without being affected by; in spite of.

Despite my successes or failures or stupidity or brilliance or fear or stress or grace or achievement, He remains good.

Our behavior does not affect the goodness of God.

This also means our behavior does not affect the goodness of God *to each other.*

Consider: Other people can't prevent God's goodness to you. Someone else cannot block what He wants to do for you.

I know all the things you do, and I have opened a door for you that no one can close. Revelation 3:8

Your blessings do not threaten my blessings. And vice versa.

Our failures do not offend God and restrict His goodness. Jesus made sure of that for us.

For God made Christ, who never sinned, to be the offering for our sin, so that we could be made right with God through Christ. 2 Corinthians 5:21

God doesn't pull away and give the cold shoulder when we don't get everything right.

He remains *forever good.*

Despite how things look at the moment. The voices you're hearing. The bill that's looming. The shoe that's dropping.

He is good *despite. Without being affected by; in spite of.*

You've probably heard all the clichés.

"Life is hard. God is good."

"God is good, all the time. All the time, God is good."

I hate clichés. Mostly because they usually pop out of the mouth of some well-meaning Christian at the time when we least need a cliché to trivialize what we're dealing with.

"She's in a better place."

"Keep your chin up."

Grrr.

But for real. If God is good...all the time... then, whatever is bugging you is *somehow* being used by God to develop you. If God is good, and His goodness has no limit, then my slice of the pie doesn't mean less pie for you.

Her opportunity doesn't mean less chance for me.

His job success doesn't translate to a lid on yours.

That guy who is *determined* to make your life difficult might change *if he believed that God is good to him too.*

When we forget that God is actively working His goodness on the periphery of our lives, we live in fear.

When we believe that He is unfailingly, unstoppably, unflinchingly, unwaveringly, determinedly, brilliantly GOOD, there is LITERALLY nothing to worry about. (Shall we start an adverb list next?)

The enemy can throw all his darts. He can try to whisper worries. He can threaten and roar all he wants.

But when you shout back, MY GOD IS GOOD, and embrace ALL that that means for you, YOU WIN.

Whatever comes up today, stand by your desk and recite it with me. Repeat it over and over so you never forget it[2]:

I believe my God is good. Aboard about above across after against...

You can't see it. The fear will grip your heart like a baby fist around a handful of hair.

I believe my God is good. Along among around at before behind below beneath beside between...

Fight back.

I believe my God is good. Beyond but by down during except for from in inside into...

Stand up straight.

I believe my God is good. Like near off of on over past since through throughout to toward...

Stomp your foot.

I believe MY GOD IS GOOD. Under underneath until up upon...

Say it like you mean it, dammit!

I BELIEVE MY GOD IS GOOD. WITH WITHIN WITHOUT!!!

We're in this together. We'll yell it together. We will not forget. We will not lose the words. We're filled up and fully equipped and *we know everything we need to know: OUR GOD IS GOOD.*

[1] *Yes, I did type that list (mostly) from memory. No, it doesn't include all the prepositions in existence. But hey, I'm 41 and I still remember the words. So there.*

[2] *I would like to thank Miss Parker. And Mrs. Holcomb. And Mr. Underwood. And all those teachers who made us recite stuff over and over in order to remember it. It worked.*

.

57

Fight On

◆

Some hours feel like a fight for sanity.

Traffic, broken things, attitude problems, splinters.

Some days feel like a fight for survival.

Schedules, interruptions, bad news, "those" people.

And some seasons feel like a fight for your life.

Illness, fatigue, confusion, change.

Life feels like one fight after another. The struggle – legitimately – is real.

If you have no struggle, no fight to face, you are either hiding or lying.

And both hiding and lying are a fight, so you remain a fighter for whatever it is you're after.

If you're going to live to fight another day, you might as well fight for something that matters.

To free the real you that's inside.

To love yourself: your body, your wiring.

To free someone else.

To create.

To forgive.

To win against the enemy of your destiny.

I'm generally an optimist with barrels of faith and good news to share.

But in this moment today, I just want you to know if you're weary from the fight, IT'S OK.

In the fight, you live.

You are real.

Dig in and stay in.

It's only an hour, a day, or a season, but it's now, and it's yours, so own it.

Feel the feels. Talk to someone. Ask for help. Fight alone. Grab onto faith. Whatever.

Just don't be surprised there's a fight or live in denial.

The fight IS what it IS.

And in the fight, you learn, stretch, grow; you become who you're being created to be.

Fight on. You got this.

58

My Desperate Prayer

◆

I'm just going to get really honest here for a minute.

I don't get super sad very often. I lean more toward super angry. Once in awhile, when someone does or says something just *so wrong* to me, the anger wells up and I can't find it in myself to even think straight. The thoughts in my mind are so overwhelming that I feel paralyzed to fight them.

It's like I have that little cartoon angel on one shoulder and the little cartoon devil on the other, except it feels very real, and the devil has this grip on my ear that is so strong, there's nothing I can do! I imagine all the things I want to spew at the person – ungracious, angry words that would do a lot of damage to that relationship or to the reputation of Jesus that I carry.

When this happens, all I can do is helplessly call out the name of Jesus until I'm capable of saying/doing more to fight whatever battle is going on up in my head. Remember, the power represented in the name of Jesus beaks through lies and strongholds and causes evil to run crying.

> *Therefore, God elevated him to the place of highest honor and gave him the name above all other names, that at the name of Jesus every knee should bow, in heaven [the angelic realm] and on earth [people] and under the earth [the demonic realm]... Philippians 2:9-10*

So I'll say,

Jesus!

And I'll get a feeling/thought that says, *No!* Because I do not want to give up the anger I'm feeling—you know the kind—where I firmly believe I have a right to be angry.

So I say it again,

Jesus! Help me!

There's a prayer that the ancient saints used to recite, called the Jesus Prayer. There is a reference to the use of this prayer as early as AD 600.[1] I use this prayer sometimes when I just can't summon the will to do anything else.

Lord Jesus Christ, Son of God, have mercy on me, a sinner!

Lord Jesus Christ, Son of God, have mercy on me, a sinner!

This prayer encompasses the truth that we need for God to help us.

Lord Jesus Christ: This confesses the Lordship of Jesus (He's in charge) over my life.

Son of God: This makes it clear which Jesus I'm talking about (as opposed to referring to *hay-sus*, the Mexican guy down the street).

Have mercy on me: Come help me!

A sinner: I'm being overwhelmed with sinful thoughts right now that will lead to sinful behavior!

Lord Jesus Christ, Son of God, have mercy on me, a sinner!

I'll repeat this, usually with every slow breath in and slow breath out, until the power of Jesus has broken the grip of the enemy force. (I know when this happens because I feel strong enough to do battle again and pray on my own.) I then proceed to banish that angry spirit and invite the Holy Spirit's peace and joy back into my situation and emotions.

Alone, we are powerless to fight. But when we invoke the name of Jesus, a power that exceeds all that exists in the universe fights on our behalf.

But you belong to God, my dear children. You have already won a victory... because the Spirit who lives in you is greater than the spirit who lives in the world. 1 John 4:4

---

[1]McGinn, Bernard (2006). *The Essential Writings of Christian Mysticism.* New York: Modern Library. p. 125.

59

I Mean, What's the Worst That Could Happen?

————◆————

Do you ever have moments when you look at someone's life or hear their story and think, *God let them down*?

Does their struggle strike a little splinter of fear in your heart as you think, *what if He does that to me?*

The world has an awful lot of really good people who have really sh!%*y situations. People who follow God to the best of their ability and still struggle with major issues.

It looks like they are doing all (or most of) the right things, and He just decided to let their lives get all jacked up.

Sometimes I see that—like a pastor's wife I know who is fighting cancer—and if I dwell on it, I get nervous. What if God allows my life to go through something devastating for His arbitrary reasons? I trust Him to meet my needs and take care of me. But because I'm a firm believer in God's sovereignty (He rules), and I know my life is all about His purposes, not mine, I have this underlying fear that He might suddenly just choose not to bless me, or to suddenly throw my human stupidity in my face and let my life fall apart.

BUT.

I cannot know God's view of someone else's situation. I cannot know their hearts or lives or the inner workings of their world... or even how they will view their time of hardship when they come out on the other side.

I can't base my view of how God works on someone else's experience. ONLY MINE.

And in my experience, He has always been faithful. In my experience, even if something looked like a loss, it was for a "better." The uncertainties and struggles and worrisome times when I was certain it would all hit the fan... those are such pale memories now, in light of the *for-my-good* outcomes on the other side.

And we know that God causes everything to work together for the good of those who love God and are called according to his purpose for them. Romans 8:28

So each day I choose to only look at His faithfulness in *my* life. I will not let someone else's situation strike fear in my heart... a fear that God will randomly strike my life with chaos, want, or loss.

He has ALWAYS been good to me. I have never gone hungry or homeless or shoeless. I have never gone bankrupt or been seriously ill.

I am willing to go through the above, if God calls me to, but based on my personal experience and His consistent track record in my life, I can stay in faith and claim the promise found in Scripture:

Seek first His kingdom [His rule in my life] and His righteousness, all these things [such as clothing, food, shelter] will be added to me as well. (Matthew 6:33, my paraphrase)

What's the worst that could happen? Well, I could die and go to heaven. Paul discusses this in his letter to the Philippians.

For I fully expect and hope that I will never be ashamed, but that I will continue to be bold for Christ, as I have been in the past. And I trust that my life will bring honor to Christ, whether I live or die. For to me, living means living for Christ, and dying is even better. But if I live, I can do more fruitful work for Christ. So I really don't know which is better. I'm torn between two desires: I long to go and be with Christ, which would be far better for me. But for your sakes, it is better that I continue to live. Knowing this, I am convinced that I will remain alive so I can continue to help all of you grow and experience the joy of your faith. Philippians 1:20-25

To live for Christ: great. You're in the care of your good Father, and He uses your life to help people meet Him and find faith.

To pass on to heaven: also great. You're in the care of your good Father, and He will use your story to help people meet Him and find faith.

It's an elevated view of life and death that requires us to give fear the finger and keep our eyes on Jesus. We're going to be OK.

60

Ain't No Shame

———◆———

So now there is no condemnation for those who belong to Christ Jesus.
Romans 8:1

When Holland was a toddler, she grew accustomed to Braden (her older brother by four years) yelling at her when she did something bad.

"Ho-LLAAAAAND!" He would begin, and then proceed to tell her what she did wrong.

Over time, Braden became the voice in her head that accused her when she would spill something or break something or commit whatever little toddler sin she slipped into. And instead of Braden yelling, we would hear her own little voice float from wherever she was: "Ho-YAAAAND!" She would accuse herself, effectively cuing us in on something gone wrong in her little world.

We all have that accusatory voice in our heads, don't we? Maybe it started with a critical teacher or friend gone mean. A religious person or parent suffering from her own guilt. Those words, those accusations became the voices so familiar that they became our own.

Instead of the accusation coming from outside, we own it.

I'm so dumb. I can't get that right.

People expect so much from me.

I made a mistake. I hurt them.

No one will ever like me for who I am.

I have to perform just so.

It has to be this way, or I'm a failure.

I'm broken. Not worthy.

The voices are unique for each of us, but common to all. Accusations, condemnation. They are the brilliant tools of Satan, our enemy, to hold us hostage and keep us from twirling. He is actually called "the accuser" (Revelation 12:10). But as God's girls, we no longer live as victims of the condemning voices. We shout them down with truth.

There is NO CONDEMNATION for you!

God does not condemn you. He doesn't point His finger and accuse you. So don't pull a toddler-Holland and accuse yourself either. When those sneaky voices try to pull your focus off Jesus and on to your perceived failures, rip your eyes away and put them back on Him and this truth: There is NO CONDEMNATION for me. I have made mistakes. I will continue to do so. But I am not condemned. I am not bad. I am loved by God. Jesus makes sure of that.

Say it aloud. Write it on your mirror. Write it on your face.

There is NO CONDEMNATION for me because of Jesus.

There is NO CONDEMNATION for me because of Jesus!

61

Breathe

———◆———

I'm into yoga. I have a YouTube instructor that I like, so most days I pick a video that addresses my need (yoga for sciatica lately). I unroll my mat on my bedroom floor, light a candle, shut my door, ("I'm doing YOGA! Leave me ALONE!"), and stretch and breathe. It is SO good for my soul to pay attention to my tension, remember I'm loved by my Father, and connect with His Spirit in me as I slow down and do something that is healthy for my body. Breathe. Stretch. Release the tension. Focus on Jesus and His peace. Breeeeeaaaathe.

***

Ever feel like you're getting sucked in to a place you really shouldn't be, and you feel powerless to stop? Anger starts in your belly and begins to rise as a flood of words you know you'll regret later, *but are so true right now,* erupt from your mouth, and you have this out-of-body experience where you are watching yourself behave like a classless reality-TV chick, and you just. can't. stop unloading on your husband.

What, is it just me?

Only *you* know your own trigger points and areas of defeat, but you're not alone in this.

I have good news for you today: You have the power of the life-giving Spirit of God! What is so powerful about God's Spirit? Connect it back to Jesus. The Spirit of God defeated the ultimate power on earth: death. Jesus died for us, but you know the Easter story. He came back to life. *Some kind of power* had to come into play to pull that off.

Now imagine yourself in your scenario of temptation. You're face-to-face with the person. Or you're staring at the computer, your finger on the mouse. *I shouldn't do this again. But I always do. I can't stop.* But you know that later you will have regret and the condemning voices will start.

And then from some place deep inside, you feel the warmth of the Spirit of God speaking. *You don't need this. It's not good for you. You're loved. You're strong with My power.* You take a deep breath. It is the breath of God that gave you life and continues to sustain you.

Then the Lord God formed the man from the dust of the ground. He breathed the breath of life into the man's nostrils, and the man became a living person. Genesis 2:7

In the struggling moments, let your breath remind you of His Spirit in you.

And because you belong to him, the power of the life-giving Spirit has freed you from the power of sin that leads to death. Romans 8:2

Notice the verse says, *"has freed you from the power of sin..."* Not, "you're being freed," or "will one day be freed." The power of God has (past-tense) already freed you from the power of sin. The challenge today is to believe it and breathe it and live it out.

The breath of LIFE is in you.

Breeeeeaaaathe.

62

Think About That

———◆———

I'm feeling pretty good about myself today. I'm going to weigh myself. After I use the bathroom. And remove all my clothes. And my watch. And glasses.

Instead of a loss… the &^%$ scale registered a 1.5 pound gain.

My thoughts swiftly spiral downward. Around the bowl and down the hole, as we say.

I will never lose weight. I can't even stop gaining! I suck at this. I'm destined to be fat. I hit 40, and my body quit even TRYING.

The negativity accelerates.

It's not worth it. Screw this.

Then the thoughts move toward an action plan.

I need a waffle right now. Also bacon.

Not exactly the action plan that will get me closer toward my goal of feeling good about my body.

> *Those who are dominated by the sinful nature think about sinful things, but those who are controlled by the Holy Spirit think about things that please the Spirit. So letting your sinful nature control your mind leads to death. But letting the Spirit control your mind leads to life and peace. Romans 8:5-6*

Quick, who wants *life and peace*? Raise your hand! Yeah, me too.

It all starts IN YOUR MIND. I cannot stress this enough. The entire battle for your peace and sanity and life is waged IN YOUR MIND. It is the battlefield upon which life and death, light and dark, joy and depression, all the struggles that mark your life, are fought.

This verse says to let the Spirit control your mind, so you think toward life, not death. This is WAY easier said right now in this moment, than done in an hour when your boss does that annoying thing. Again. And the thoughts in your head start to deteriorate.

So here's what I've got for you today: if you want a healthy, peace-filled mind, you have to *think about* what you are *thinking about*. Notice your internal dialogue. What are the thoughts bouncing around in there? It's a Big Freakin' Deal. Here's your assignment: Think about what you're thinking about. Notice.

It will take some effort and discipline, so ask God to help you notice your thoughts today. Maybe put an X or something on your hand to remind you to pay attention to your thoughts and whether they sound like something coming from the Spirit of God, leading to life... or somewhere else, leading to yucky results.

63

Where's This Train Headed?

———◆———

I was standing at the kitchen sink (yet again), washing dishes and cleaning the kitchen (alone, yet again). Eric was on the couch on his laptop (yet again) blissfully unaware that this train of thought was chugging through my mind.

I'm doing this alone again. I really wish he'd help me. He's sitting there while I do all this work. And this is after I've already done the work of cooking and serving dinner!

Note: the circumstances were true. Admitting them was OK, but then this came next: *He's sitting there because he just assumes I'll clean the kitchen. I'm just a housekeeper. If he actually cared about me, he'd help me. But he doesn't.*

Choo choo! All aboard to Crazyville!

Everything in our life is about ME serving HIM. Me helping him accomplish stuff. Me enabling him to be successful. And he doesn't care about my needs. And it goes on and on until poor, unsuspecting Eric walks through the kitchen and I launch a dramatic verbal attack worthy of an Oscar.

Do any of my sisters connect with that story? Some chick at work looks at you funny as you pass in the hall, and you think, *Gah, I knew she didn't like me. She's mad that I got assigned lead on that project. She's so jealous and insecure. I'm just going to shut her out...* and really she was just in a rush to the restroom. But your train of thought will take you to Damaged-Relationship Land so fast!

As you get in the habit of thinking about what you're thinking about, it's a great idea to pause and look down the tracks your train of thought is following. Where do they lead? If you keep thinking like this, what's the result?

If you think about how much you hate your job, will you end up working hard and being successful, or will you undermine your own ability to succeed?

If you think about how difficult your child is, will your eyes light up when he walks into the room, so he feels safe? Or will you automatically be annoyed as soon as you see him?

If you think about how small your house is, will you be grateful for it and make it as functional and beautiful as possible, or will you resent it and let it slide?

EVERY. SINGLE. TRAIN. runs on tracks that lead somewhere. Don't jump on without thinking about the destination.

64

Basic White Sauce

———◆———

This is a GREAT recipe to have in your back pocket.

Melt 2 tablespoons of butter in a saucepan over medium heat.

After it's melted, use a wire whisk to stir in 2 tablespoons of flour.

Keep stirring until a rough paste (roux) is formed. (The flour soaks up the butter, and the floury flavor is cooked out.)

Stir in 1 cup of milk, and keep stirring until a creamy sauce is formed. Add more or less milk (or even water or broth) to adjust the consistency as desired.

Add salt and pepper.

This sauce will be bland because it's designed as a base for other uses.

Uses (among a million others):

Add chicken bouillon to make cream of chicken soup that you can add to recipes like Potatoes, Kraut & Sausage and other casseroles that call for cream soup.

Stir in shredded cheddar and pour over noodles for homemade mac & cheese. For more awesomeness, put it all in a baking dish and sprinkle with crushed crackers stirred in melted butter and more cheese. Bake until toasty.

Stir in shredded cheddar and cooked broccoli for broccoli/cheese soup. (May want to add extra liquid.)

Stir in Parmesan, a squeeze of lemon juice, and some garlic salt for alfredo sauce. Add some cubed cream cheese if you want to increase your chances of a heart attack.

Pour a thin stream into boiling broth, stirring constantly, to thicken your gravy.

Add lots of pepper for Southern-style pepper gravy for biscuits, mashed potatoes, or breaded fried chicken breasts.

Make it in the pan you just used to cook ground sausage and then stir some of the sausage back in at the end. Serve over buttered biscuits.

Chop up and stir in that super-cheap Carl Buddig lunch meat (beef). Add some peas, serve over toast. We had this a *lot* when I was a kiddo. My mom is legendary for making meals that cost pennies.

65

How To Lighten Up

———◆———

Part 1: Buy Less Stuff

It is very difficult to twirl with open arms and a generous heart if your life is weighed down with Too Much. Too much stuff to purchase, store, and maintain will weigh you down.

There are two parts to this "too much stuff" problem. The first is getting, and the second is not getting rid of it. I once talked to a woman who said, "I love to shop! I go buy a bunch of stuff, and even if I have to return it the next day, it was worth it, because I still got that thrill from finding it and bringing it home."

Maybe it is a comfort thing. Like comforting yourself with food or alcohol/drugs, buying things is a way for many of us to fill an empty place in our hearts. If this is you, consider for a moment why you shop and acquire so much. Do you do it because:

- you feel good about yourself when you make a purchase,
- you need to have what "everyone else" has,
- your life feels out of control, and this is something that's just for *you*, that you can control,
- you feel entitled, thinking, *I earn a paycheck! I deserve to spend a*

little on me!, or
- you simply crave *more*?

I totally understand the temporary high of getting something new, but I also know that an unbalanced approach to acquiring stuff leads *away*, not *toward,* the destiny God has for you. It is a selfish, greedy habit that makes possessions an idol in your life.

Let me ask you a question (btw, this is a great question to ask in any area of your life): what is the fruit of this behavior? What is at the end of the path you're walking? Excess? Credit debt? Guilt for overspending? Conflict with your husband? Lack in other areas, like an inability to pay your bills or be generous to others?

If you're a bargain shopper, you might be addicted to the thrill of the hunt for the next deal. I knew a woman who could find *anything* at a bargain price. It's like she had some kind of gift, honed over the years, for finding deals. And she did it constantly. Online, in stores, home parties; wherever shopping could be done. The fruit of her behavior? Her beautiful home was full of clutter. Her basement was full. There was stuff everywhere, and it was rarely clean. Even her teenage children were disgusted by how much crap she held onto. They were choking in excess, and it seemed like she valued her possessions more than her family.

We never had much money when I was growing up, so I learned to be a bargain shopper. I LOVE thrift stores, yard sales, and clearance racks, and for a while, I did the extreme-coupon thing. There's just something thrilling about paying way less for something than everyone else. Because the "bargain" part of the shopping keeps me free of the "spending money" guilt, I can shop more. But the result of this is *still* a cluttered house, overstuffed dressers and closets, and a preoccupation with finding more!

I think extreme-couponing is awesome, except for three things:

- People tend to buy way more than they need, creating massive unnecessary stockpiles (some give it away, which is noble).
- It would appear that the time spent preparing for a shopping trip may be at the expense of what should be higher priorities.
- It nurtures an obsession with getting stuff. More coupons, more deals, more stuff. Fear of missing a sale or deal becomes a problem too.

I still enjoy shopping for bargains, but here's how I generally go about it (this is what works for *me*. You have to figure out what's a good system for *you*):

I try to only shop when I need something. (For example, I decided that a second waffle maker would be good to have, since I make roughly 30 waffles at a time and freeze them.) This gives me a reason to hit the thrift store.

As I enter the store, I pray that God will show me what I should buy. *(God, show me a waffle maker!)*

If the item isn't there, I'll browse, but only for things I need. No waffle maker? I'll check and see if they have a rug I need for the front porch. However, I *try* to stay out of the purse section unless I *need* a purse and am prepared to part with one I already have. (Full disclosure: at present, I have an abundance of shoes. I didn't say I'm perfect at this. The general concept is what we're going after here.)

And sometimes God shows me something awesome. Like a dish that goes with my antique set. If I find something that's only half-awesome, I won't buy it. I don't want to fill my life with half-awesome junk. It's a lifelong growth process that I'm still working on.

Did you know that Jesus wants your life to be awesome? *[Satan's] purpose is to steal and kill and destroy. My [Jesus'] purpose is to give them a rich and satisfying life. John 10:10*

You know, Satan is sneaky and tries to mess with our thinking by getting us to focus on the wrong things. Well, here's one of the ways he does this: He gets us to accept half-awesome stuff instead of waiting for God's awesomeness.

Do you ever cram your life full of as much mediocre as you can, hoping that collectively it will become awesome — but it doesn't? It's just a whole lotta mediocre. It's like eating a food item that isn't really good, but somehow you think if you keep eating, it will get better.

I can't tell you how many times I've bought something that I thought I could "make work", only to invest more time and money into it than if I had just waited until I had enough cash or God provided for me the perfectly "right" thing.

Recently I received a text from a fellow bargain-shopping friend. It said, "At the store with a gift card. Can't get out of the clearance racks. Please tell me it's OK to buy something *not* on clearance." I read it to Eric (who cares about my friend too). He grabbed my phone and texted back, "Get out of clearance! You're more valuable than that! Go buy something you love!"

When we're locked into a thought process of *get the most for my money,* we're OK with buying three mediocre items from clearance that we can "make work" instead of just one really nice full-price item. Sometimes we need permission to accept a full-size blessing from God, and not be stuck in a mediocre mentality.

Action step: Re-evaluate the thinking behind your shopping. Find one area you might be out of balance in the acquiring of stuff. Do you want to make a change? Great! Make a plan.

66

How To Lighten Up

———————◆———————

Part 2: Get Rid of Stuff

Several years ago at The Crossing, we taught a series called SHED. During that series, we challenged people to get rid of stuff, paring their personal belongings down to 100 items or fewer. This was an eye-opener, as I realized how much stuff I had! Last year, we moved to a home with roughly half the square footage we previously had. We gave away or threw away a ton of stuff, and we haven't even missed it! In fact, I stubbornly held on to a few things that (one year later) I still have not used.

The Bible talks about *stuff* in Matthew 6:19: *Don't store up treasures here on earth, where moths eat them and rust destroys them, and where thieves break in and steal.*

These are the three things I notice.

Uno: the words *store up.* This would imply having more than you need, and stockpiling.

Dos: *moths eat them.* When I think of moths eating things, I think of moth balls. Which makes me think of grandma's house, which (once again) includes *storing* things that are unused, requiring moth balls to keep the moths from eating holes in it as it lies there, pointlessly taking up space.

Tres: *rust destroys them.* This, once again, is referring to something that sits unused, or deteriorates for lack of care. If you don't use it, and you don't care enough about it to maintain it, it's probably just *stuff you are storing.*

Have you seen the History Channel show "American Pickers"? These two guys, Mike and Frank, drive around the country, mostly to people's homes, and dig around in their junk to find "treasure" they can sell for a profit. So many of these people's yards or barns are just loaded with rusty garbage, yet often, when Mike or Frank will offer to buy an item, the owners will refuse. It's a piece of junk they will never use, but they just can't part with it.

It's sad, really, but sometimes it's me. And I'm guessing, sometimes it's you.

Why do we store things? I can think of a few reasons we may hold onto stuff.

It's sentimental. Why do we keep our children's baby teeth? It's a collection of BONES from their HEADS. If you think about it, it's really gross. Yet we keep them to...what? Remind us of when they cut those teeth on Gerber biscuits? When they bit us while breastfeeding (OW!)? I don't know why we do this! OK, that's a kind of silly example. Here's more: my high school volleyball jersey. The resort map from our Cancun trip. Eric's graduation hat from college. Well, maybe those are understandable. But the ragged sweatshirt that's "sentimental" simply because you've had it for twelve years? The legitimately HORRIBLE wall plaque your great aunt gave you?

Let's separate sentiment from guilt. If you'll feel guilty for getting rid of it, I hereby absolve you. Not a single one of your children will come to you one day and ask for their baby teeth back. Your great aunt in Heaven doesn't care if you donate her plaque to Goodwill. And your sweatshirt needs to be burned. I'm not even going to try to make you feel better about that. If it's truly sentimental, and you think generations to come will take pleasure or pride in an item, keep it. I have a cedar chest in which I keep sentimental items: my first Barbie (she's naked), my cheerleading sweater, our kids' baby blankets, and all of Eric's and my journals. That's about it. If it can't fit in one chest, it's probably too much sentiment.

It was expensive. In one of my business classes in college, I learned a concept that goes like this,: "Sunk costs are irrelevant." Meaning, don't continue using something you hate or that doesn't work right for you just because it cost you X amount of money. That money's long gone, whether you use the item or not. Keeping the item doesn't get your money back.

"But Kelly, I have to wear these shoes! They were expensive!"

"They hurt your feet."

"Yeah, but I paid so much for them, I have to get my money's worth!"

"But they HURT YOUR FEET." Get rid of the shoes. If you can, sell them and get some of your money back. But don't keep something you hate just because of the price you paid. Continuing to keep or use something is simply costing you more: it's costing your comfort, your peace, your pleasure. Ditch it.

I might need it! Often, we're motivated by fear that if we get rid of something, we might need it in the future... and then we'll be screwed! We see this behavior in those who went through the Great Depression. My grandma doesn't waste anything that could be useful (i.e., Cool Whip containers and egg cartons) and doesn't get rid of anything unless it's to someone who needs it and is certain to use it. Admittedly, sometimes this comes in handy. A couple years ago, I was visiting my grandparents, and I unexpectedly needed an, um, feminine product. Off went Grandma to some dark corner of a drawer, and she came back with an ancient maxi pad. Enclosed with it was a ten-cents-off coupon that expired sometime around 1973 (I'm not exaggerating)! Regardless of age, it did the job, and I was grateful.

However, we can't live our lives hoarding everything we have in case we might need it one day. For about 15 years, I kept a food processor we received as a wedding gift. I think I used it about five times. But I kept it, thinking I might need it. I donated it during our SHED process, and I have probably missed it once, when I needed to shred some cabbage. I know it's hard to believe, but a good kitchen knife shredded that cabbage just fine. (And made me feel like a legit chef chopping vegetables.) You know what else? If I decide to do some major food-processing, I can go to the thrift store and buy another one for a couple of bucks! In the meantime, I don't have a food processor taking up space and getting dusty in my kitchen or closet.

"I might need it!" is fear, really. Shake it off. Ask yourself this: "Is this something I *will* need, or something I *might* need?" There's a difference. Proverbs 6 talks about the ant who wisely stores up in summer what he'll need for winter. Proverbs 31 extols the woman who doesn't "fear winter" because her family has all they need. It's wise to prepare for the future. Keeping the air pump for a mattress you no longer have might not be necessary. Philippians 4:19 says that God will supply all your needs. So, conceivably, if at some point in the future, you actually *need* this item, God will make sure you get it.

All that to say this: Twirling is tough if you're always reaching out to grab more stuff and hugging everything you have to your chest. Free yourself up.

Be thankful you have what you need, and don't continually pursue more.

But also, lighten your load and let some stuff go, OK?

Lighten up! It's false guilt that's forcing you to store stuff.

Lighten up! You already spent the money. Don't torture yourself with something you hate.

Lighten up! Your good God will supply all your needs if you'll trust Him to take care of you.

This, my friend, will free you to twirl.

67

Characteristics of a Peaceful Mind

———◆———

How's it going? Are you remembering to think about what you're thinking about? Are you noticing whether your trains of thought are headed to Crazyville instead of Peaceland? Does your inner dialogue indulge in negativity or crankiness leading to sadness, or graciousness leading to joy?

If it isn't going so awesome, it's OK. We're learning some tools today.

> And now, dear brothers and sisters, one final thing. Fix your thoughts on what is true, and honorable, and right, and pure, and lovely, and admirable. Think about things that are excellent and worthy of praise. Keep putting into practice all you learned and received from me—everything you heard from me and saw me doing. Then the God of peace will be with you. Philippians 4:8-9

The apostle Paul wrote this letter to some believers, and he wanted them to learn how to live in peace: think right thoughts! Here's his list with a few follow up questions to help evaluate whether your train of thought is running the right direction.

Is what you're thinking about...

- True? (Is it cold, hard, truth—or simply your speculation?)

- Honorable? (Does the thought give honor to the other person? Remember, we give honor to every person because Christ gave His life for them too.)

- Right? (Do you have a right to think this way? Jesus gave you grace. Are you rightfully extending that grace to another?)

- Pure? (Purity means undefiled. Purity of heart has been defined as being about ONE thing: living out God's destiny for you. Do these thoughts defile the one thing your heart should be purely about?)

- Lovely? (Is that thought full of love?)

- Admirable? (If you held that thought up for others to see, would they admire it, or would you be embarrassed?)

- Excellent? (Is this really the best you can do?)

- Worthy of praise? (If you say the thought aloud, can you praise God with the next breath?)

If your thoughts fail to meet these qualifications, Scripture tells us to not let those trains keep running! We need to stop them and switch tracks.

...we take captive every thought to make it obedient to Christ. 2 Corinthians 10:5b (NIV)

When you elevate your thinking to goodness and purity and love, you will elevate the way you live. An open mind to the guidance of Christ opens your life to His peace and joy. That train can only go someplace good.

68

God's Stamp on Your Soul

◆────────────◆

A couple years ago, my sisters and I got matching tattoos of "klina birds". (Don't bother Googling *klina bird*. It doesn't exist. It's from a song we sang in the car as little kids.) Chrissie's and mine are on the outside of our wrists; Katie's is on her foot.

Many tattoos that women choose are placed in, shall we say, *less than public* places on our bodies. We like to be strategic about who is going to see that stamp, and when. So it's a kind of private stamp, and only sometimes does it see the light of day. I believe that God has stamped an image of Himself on the soul of every woman. Like a secret tattoo, it's not often seen, and this is because we have an enemy of our souls who does his best to distort, hide, and lie about the stamp God's printed on us. So let's shine some light on that tattoo, shall we?

First, a foundational truth. God designed women in His image.

When God created human beings, he made them to be like himself. He created them male and female, and he blessed them and called them "human". Genesis 5:1-2

God is referred to as "He" throughout Scripture, so often people assume that men are His favorite, or only men reflect the image of God; women were an afterthought. But according to this verse, it was His plan all along to make a second human. He said, "OK, I'm going to make humans in my image. This one is the male. I will stamp on him the image of my masculine qualities. This one is female. I will stamp on her the image of my feminine qualities. Together, they make up a complete picture of me."

I can live with that. Now let's look at the feminine qualities He stamped on us, and how we can live them out.

Women wear God's stamp by being the savior of man.

Yes, you read that right. The savior of man. Here's proof. God made Adam, took one look, and said, "It is not good." (OK, that wasn't the whole sentence.)

It is not good for the man to be alone. I will make a helper who is just right for him. Genesis 2:18

If you're offended by the idea that you were designed to spend your life being some guy's assistant, raise your hand. Yeah, I'm with ya, sister. The great thing is that when we look at the Hebrew word for *helper,* it's *ezer kenegdo,* which means, *to rescue/save/to be strong.*

Ah, yes. That's much better. The verse says, "I will make a savior/rescuer who is just right for him." Nice. That should make you feel a bit better. You were not an afterthought, created to do your man's dirty work; his secretary, cook, and housekeeper. You were made to be the strong savior and rescuer of man. This sounds almost...well, noble!

But now I have some icing for your self-image cake. The word God used for woman in that verse (*ezer kenegdo)* is the SAME WORD the psalmist used for God Himself in scripture!

The Lord is my light and my salvation [ezer kenegdo]. Psalm 27:1

Whoa. Now it's a little scary. God stamped on our souls the calling to be the savior of man. Question: If God placed the calling to be the savior or rescuer of a man on the soul of every woman, should it surprise us that some girls are boy-crazy? Nope. We're wired to be that way. It's like the moment the chromosomes did their thing, identifying a chick as a chick, a homing beacon beeped on, and began her lifelong search for the man for whom she will be the "just-right savior." Woman is wired to rescue man.

So what do we rescue a man *from*? Well, maybe this is just speculation, but I'd say three things. First, *loneliness*. The verse says, *It is not good for man to be alone...* meaning, God did not design humans to live in isolation. He wired us for connection and community, so when a woman chooses to marry a man, she rescues him from loneliness.

Second, I think a woman rescues a man from *himself*. Face it: left to themselves, dudes are wired for self-destruction. They eat poorly, fail to bathe, and do dumb things that singe their eyebrows off. A woman comes along and helps him eat better, inspires him to bathe (no shower, no sex?), and reminds him to flip the breaker before messing with the wiring. Woman rescues man from his own stupidity. (On the off chance that a guy is reading this book, please accept the permission slip my husband gave me to say that.)

Third, a woman is wired to rescue a man from a life of *insignificance*. When Jack Nicholson told Helen Hunt in the famous scene from *As Good As It Gets*, "You make me want to be a better man," I think he echoed men everywhere when they find "just the right *ezer kenegdo*". A good woman makes a man want to be better. A good woman will inspire a man to work hard to provide for her. A good woman will inspire a man to fight to defend her. A good woman will link arms with a man and walk beside him as they make the world a better place: maybe having children and bringing them up in faith, serving others, and pointing people to Jesus. A good woman rescues a man from an insignificant life, gives him something to live for, and helps him accomplish his dreams.

Loneliness. Man's own stupidity. A life of insignificance.

Who else rescues mankind from these?

Who else says, "I will never leave you...you're never alone?"

Who else says, "I will forgive your past and lead you into an abundant life?"

Who else says, "Walk with me, and I will help you do great things?"

Jesus.

When you live out your design of being the rescuer of man, you're reflecting the very nature of Jesus Christ to the world. This is part of the image of God that is stamped on your soul. Savior of man.

You are not desperate.
You are not weak.
You are not inferior.
You are not a victim.

You have the internal wiring of a savior, patterned after THE Savior of mankind. You've got a high calling to live out once you realize what your Creator says about you.

You are *ezer kenegdo.*

With the nature of a savior.

Never let anyone tell you you're less-than. Never believe the lie that you have a secondary role in the world.

You carry the image of God Himself into every situation and relationship, so listen to His Spirit and let Him empower you to live out His nature with quiet confidence.

***

Linus Larrabee:

So, that really is a beautiful name. How did you get it?

Sabrina Fairchild:

My father's reading. It's in a poem.

Linus:

Oh?

Sabrina:

"Sabrina fair, listen where thou art sitting under the glassy, cool, translucent wave, in twisted braids of lilies knitting the loose train of thy amber-dropping hair."

Linus:

[pause] So, your little poem - what does it mean?

Sabrina:

It's the story of a water sprite who saved a virgin from a fate worse than death.

Linus:

And Sabrina's the virgin.

Sabrina:

[quietly] Sabrina's the savior.[1]

---

[1]Doran, L. (Exec. Producer), & Pollock, S. (Director). (1995). *Sabrina* [Motion Picture]. United States: Paramount Pictures

69

The Benefits of Bathroom Time

———————◆———————

Eric is an idea guy. His brain is always moving really fast. Give him some alone time, and he always comes back with a bunch of new things he learned or new ideas to talk about. I ran across this in an old blog post:

I always LOVE to hear what Eric has to say after he's had some extended time with God. He is the most exciting guy I know — he always has a great idea. Seriously, whenever he says, "I've been thinking..." I drop whatever I'm doing and listen up. 'Cause it could mean we're moving to Georgia. Or Pennsylvania. Or Iowa. Or another place in Iowa. Or another place in Iowa. Or another place in Iowa. Or Minnesota. Or another place in Minnesota. Or another place in Minnesota. Or another place in Minnesota. Or another place in Minnesota. YES, these have all happened.

***

What's super funny is that he often gets good ideas when he goes to the bathroom. Ask one of our Crossing creative staff members and they'll tell you this is true. We'll be in a meeting, hashing out service ideas or something, and he'll go to the bathroom and *come back with some big idea.* Why does this happen?

Because it's hard to hear God when there are too many people talking. Get away for a few minutes, ask the Holy Spirit to give you some direction, and allow the silence so you can perceive what He might say.

The world is loud--you know that. Noise everywhere, music, advertising, words, signs, stimulus. Sometimes the only place TO find a moment of peace is when you need to pee. Unless you're in Applebee's. They have ads in the stalls.

Here's where I'm going with this. With so many words and so much noise, it is hard to hear God's *gentle whisper.* He's not one for shouting to be heard. He is big and powerful and working all around us, but when it comes to hearing His voice speaking specifically to the needs of your heart and life, you have to get alone and quiet.

> *"Go out and stand before me on the mountain," the Lord told him. And as Elijah stood there, the Lord passed by, and a mighty windstorm hit the mountain. It was such a terrible blast that the rocks were torn loose, but the Lord was not in the wind. After the wind there was an earthquake, but the Lord was not in the earthquake. And after the earthquake there was a fire, but the Lord was not in the fire. And after the fire there was the sound of a gentle whisper. When Elijah heard it, he wrapped his face in his cloak and went out and stood at the entrance of the cave. And a voice said, "What are you doing here, Elijah?"*
> *1 Kings 19:11-13*

Here's your challenge: find (or create) places of quiet in your day, so you can hear the quiet voice of God's Spirit in your heart.

The morning, before the day starts. Keep the TV, music, phone, and computer off.

The shower. I pray in the shower often. Not many distractions in there.

Your drive time. Try silence.

When you use the restroom at work, take your time!

You get it. Life is loud, but places of quiet can be found if you're purposeful.

And God will meet you wherever you choose to connect with Him.

70

To Know, Be Known, and Make Him Known

———————◆———————

A few years ago, Eric and I had dinner with a group of young people who all claimed to "not believe", whether this took the form or atheism or secular humanism or simply a choice to not have faith (and everything in between). As Eric and I asked questions and got to know the hearts and minds of these precious people whom Jesus loves, they talked about being shunned or silenced because their belief system (or lack thereof) is so uncomfortable to others.

People are afraid, they said, that these "non-believers" will try to convert them, so they are given no opportunity for dialogue. One young woman said this, "My goal isn't to convert anyone to my way of thinking. I simply want to be understood." She wanted to have someone else take the time to hear her heart, thoughts, and ideas and (even if they disagreed) to have that person accept her or at least treat her with respect for who she is.

What she really wanted, at the core of her being, was simply *to be known.*

I believe this is at the core of each of us: to be known, and then to be accepted or respected, or even rejected! Most of us who have come to a certain level of emotional maturity are OK with being rejected or disagreed with, as long as we're understood. We say, "Hey, you don't have to agree with me, but please be sure you understand what you're disagreeing with!" Being misunderstood sucks. Being misjudged and then treated like crap because of it *really* sucks!

There's no way you can ensure that everyone you come across in life will understand you perfectly or grant you respect or even, at the very least, tolerate you. It's not going to happen. So how do you get past that deep need to be known?

First, recognize that you ARE already completely known by Someone. Psalm 139 talks all about how God (your Creator) knows everything about you, including how you were woven together in the womb, what you're going to say before you say it, and what every single moment of your life will hold. And then it goes to say how "precious" are God's thoughts about you. In other words, He knows you intimately. And He loves you perfectly. Return to this truth (read that chapter in the Bible) anytime you feel alone, misunderstood, or misjudged.

Second, let go of the idea that you will ever be able to cause *everyone* to understand, like, accept, or even tolerate you. When someone says something unkind or untrue about you or looks at you funny, and you realize they've judged or misunderstood you, do you always need to explain yourself?

I confess, I've fallen into that a lot. I'll be talking with someone about my church or my family, and they'll make a statement/judgment that's off-base. All of a sudden I feel that I have to jump in and explain why their assessment of my child is incorrect or assure them that I'm not as stressed as they think I am. Ever done that? It doesn't really affect anything; I just want to put myself in the best possible light in their eyes!

Here's an example. Recently I mixed up my son's dentist appointment time *and* day two weeks in a row. I must have looked like an idiot to the receptionist. It drove me nuts that she might think I'm an airhead! But I had to just shrug my shoulders, and let it go... while laughing at myself. I didn't need to convince her that I'm normally organized, that I even have an assistant who helps me with my schedule, and that I'm not a dummy. Why does it matter? She doesn't have to like me! She doesn't have to think I'm smart! (Plus, if she's really cool [which she is], she'll laugh at me and like me anyway!)

Learn (as I am learning) to let go of your desire to control people's understanding of you. It's not your problem if someone wants to incorrectly judge you. You're known by your Creator, and He loves and accepts you 100% because Jesus covered up your flaws at the cross. Your goal in life is to please Him, and if you're walking each day guided by His Spirit, keeping "your side of the street clean", you do not have to explain yourself to others. This truth is at the very heart of your ability to twirl, without needing to look around and be sure everyone understands your version of twirling!

At the risk of sounding harsh, I'm just going to throw this out there. Sometimes you need to reject the assumption that people actually care about what you think or what you're really like! Constantly searching for opportunities to share *your* thoughts to help someone understand *you* is a self-centered approach to life, no matter what your belief system is.

The world is so much bigger than our own personal reputation. Sometimes Christians argue, "But if they misunderstand me, they'll misunderstand God!" Hear this: God is perfectly capable of managing His own reputation. I think this argument still stems from a root of pride that makes us want to always smell like roses to everyone. Let's get over that. I'll keep working on it if you will!

As Jesus-followers, we don't exist to be *known*. That happened ages ago, before the foundation of the world! We've been *known* forever! We exist to make HIM known. Rather than pointing at ourselves, our lives are lived to point to Jesus. We go through life on a mission from

God to spread the gospel (good news) of Jesus. This is our calling.

But remember the old saying that says *people don't care what you know until they know that you care.* Ask questions. Listen. Learn. Seek to know rather than be known. Seek to understand rather than be understood.

I think the biggest gift Eric and I could give to that group of young people that evening was to do just that. Rather than talk-talk-talking about our beliefs and our God, we took the very important step of hearing their stories, looking into their eyes, and, hopefully, reflecting the love and acceptance of their Creator when they looked back into ours.

71

No Memory Whatsoever

———◆———

Blog Post February 28, 2006

Holland and Aidan are home sick again. *Sigh... Deep sigh...* And here's a good question: Why doesn't Braden get sick? He's the one who goes to school every day! (Not that I want him to get sick.) But... really. Why can't we keep our little ones from getting sick every two weeks? Aidan, especially. I really believe he has some virus down in his little toes, and it makes its way up every two weeks. So I'm trying some of Aunt Julaine's suggestions. I'm soaking Aidan's feet in garlic/water. Eric says the house stinks. But, hey, I love garlic.

Eric and I were blessed to be able to spend Sunday night at the Butler House in Mankato, a B&B trip that was given to us when some of our church people submitted our names to KTIS radio during Clergy Appreciation Month. Our friend Britney's Christmas gift to us was keeping our children so we could go. WHAT A BLESSING! We drove down Sunday evening, arrived at 5:30, and were shown to our room. After dinner out, we retired to our room, and, believe it or not, we went to sleep at like 9:30. (We're really tired on Sunday nights.)

We were served a delicious breakfast in a formal dining room & enjoyed learning the history of the mansion from the host. They had a

Steinway Grand in the foyer, so I got to tickle the ivories a little bit. Ah, the joy of playing a piano that is in TUNE. (Mine is not.) We returned to Otsego and had lunch at Blackwoods (gift card), and were home before 2:00. I suppose Brit had an easier time with the kids since they were sick. More mellow that way.

Wanna hear another story of God providing? Eric (the movie buff) wanted to take the kids to see *Pink Panther*, but due to our financial project, we chose not to spend the cash (five of us to a movie costs a pretty shiny penny). On Friday, a friend called and asked if we wanted to see *Pink Panther*. I said yes, but, "We're not spending any extra money right now."

She said, "Well the reason I ask is because I have tickets for your family. I got them free, and I don't care about seeing that movie." How is THAT for God giving us the desires of our heart?! We went last night as a family. And the theater had a special with Domino's... with our movie stub, we got an XL pizza for $5 afterward. Can you believe it??!! So we had supper in the van on the way home & then put the kiddos to bed. Aidan's fever was over 102 during the night, so I gave him some ibuprofen. Holland called them in sick to school today. It was very cute. Well that's the latest with us! God Bless You!

***

That post is from ten years ago last month. When I ran across it yesterday, I could not remember any of those events. I searched and searched my memory, and I can vaguely place us in the Elk River movie theater watching the movie. I absolutely cannot recall the B&B at all. Not the piano, not the meal, nothing.

It scares the shizz out of me that I cannot remember things. This is why I play word games. I feel like I'm going to have to work really hard to keep my mind sharp, as I grow older. Also, I like word games. Years ago when I started journaling, I had no idea that that would be the only way I would remember many things.

Honestly, I'm not a super nervous person. I don't sit and worry about getting cancer or whatever, but this one gets me a little bit. *Why can I not remember things?*

Eric remembers *everything.* Every movie we've ever watched, every vacation we've had, every car we've owned. Which sucks, because anytime I've thrown careless words at him in a fight, he remembers them.

I guess the upside of my memory issue is that I get over stuff quickly. I don't hold grudges because I *literally cannot remember* what the person did to me. It's a lovely way to live, if you think about it. It's strange because I'm a pretty smart person, quick-minded with a comeback or solution. It's just some weird vortex in my brain. It's a black hole I do not understand.

It kind of reminds me of God and His approach to our sins. He's the Creator and Ruler of the Universe. Yet He just. Can't. Remember. The stuff we've done wrong.

And I will forgive their wickedness, and I will never again remember their sins. Hebrews 8:12

I—yes, I alone—will blot out your sins for my own sake and will never think of them again. Isaiah 43:25

But our High Priest [Jesus] offered himself to God as a single sacrifice for sins, good for all time. Hebrews 10:12

Because Jesus picked up the tab for our sins, God will not remember them. Can not or will not? Hmmm. I don't know. It's a black hole we cannot understand. People argue that God can do whatever He wants, otherwise He's not God, blah blah blah. But these verses say *will never*, so I think it's a choice. It's funny because we think this is a benefit for *us* that He won't remember our sins, but that Isaiah verse says it's a benefit for *Him.* He forgets our sins *for His own sake.* He probably doesn't want to remember them because they would make

Him sad, so He just won't.

I like that.

I also think it's a good model for how we should treat people who hurt us. To just choose to *not remember* their wrongs. How freeing would it be to not keep an open tab? To not review the words in your mind.? To not imagine throwing them back in their faces? To not keep it in your back pocket until a *you owe me* opportunity? Not just for his/her sake, but for yours. For your own sake, forget their mistakes and love like God loves you.

It's a lovely way to live.

72

Put Yo Glasses On

———◆———

Our son Braden turned twenty in April. He has always been an early riser like his daddy. I literally cannot recall ever waking him up for school. (Technically that means absolutely nothing; see previous chapter.) But anyway. When he was about 18 months old, he would climb out of his bed, come into our room, pick up our glasses off the nightstand, and try to hand them to us.

Here Mommy. Here Daddy. You get up now. Put yo glasses on. You get up now.

He knew that the first thing we did upon waking was to put on our glasses, so that's how he started to get us out of bed.

When you choose to believe the Bible is true, God is God, and Jesus is your Leader, you choose a new worldview. It affects how you see everything: your purpose for existing, how you treat people, how you spend your time; your habits, your spending, your thinking, your relationships.

You have the opportunity to get up every day and put on a set of lenses. To see the world through the lenses that show you God's favor and grace. His provision and blessing. His ability to help you succeed and love people and endure hard things and push through whatever you're dealing with.

If I get up in the morning and do not put on my glasses, I will spend my morning squinting. Everything will be blurry. I can't legally drive, so I won't go very far. And I'll probably get cranky and get a headache. BUT if I simply take 1.5 seconds to put my glasses on, I'm great! I can see clearly and get a good start to the day.

If you get up in the morning and do not put on your glasses of faith, it's likely that the day will be blurry. It will be hard to make wise decisions in moments of stress, you'll get cranky with people and you'll likely be all up in your head with clutter and a lack of focus. You might not go very far. BUT if you take a bit of time to say Hi to God first thing, polish up your lenses by reading some Scripture and asking God to guide your day, you'll move forward with clarity and eyes to see what He has for you.

Put yo glasses on. You get up now.

73

Ritzy Skills

———◆———

$7.49 for a can of WD-40? Pssht. I'll find something else. I look around and see plastic coffee stir-sticks. This gives me an idea. I grab two, and walk back out of the gas station in downtown St. Louis. My girlfriends look at me expectantly (probably sighing just a little bit). I tell them I decided to go with Moroccan hair oil instead. I have some and so does Diane. (We have similar frizz issues). The problem of the moment? My suitcase wheels squeak. And so do Tracy's. (They're a matching set I got for $1 each at a yard sale. SCORE! Except they squeak. Loudly. We found this out in the airport, as this was their maiden voyage in my possession.) And we are going to stay in the Ritz-freakin'-Carlton. So we try to silence the wheels by using stir sticks to apply Moroccan hair oil to the wheels. Because I'll be danged if I'm going to have some fancy bellman pull my suitcase sounding like a cat is dying inside.

I spent many of my growing-up years a chameleon. In the interest of not looking weird (one day I'll write my story and you'll understand why weird was a thing for my family), I would figure out how to adapt and fit in to unfamiliar situations, drawing the least amount of attention to myself while still feeding my need for attention and for people to like me. Trying to be "cool" and "charming," I learned to not say stupid stuff or voice strong opinions. To laugh and agree with whatever was being said. To pretend I got the joke or innuendo. To smile a lot. To participate in things I was good at (like a game of pick-up volleyball or a word game) and quietly observe things I knew would make me look stupid (like softball or anything involving running). This served me well, though it would never earn me the title of world-changer. It was a technique born not of noble social motives, but a far more primal urge to not be eaten by the herd.

These days, I use some of the same techniques to survive unfamiliar situations with (what appears to be) class. Thankfully, God has taught me some spiritual principles that are at work in me, too, which, combined with my social coping skills, help me when I am out of my element and face some anxiety. I didn't realize this until my trip to St. Louis. Here's how it went.

Three staff girls and I traveled to a conference hosted by a friend of mine. We decided to stay at the Ritz, because that's where some of the other personal guests of my friend were staying. Our ride to the conference was pre-arranged, and I didn't want to be the one they had to go pick up from Motel 6 or some other fine budget establishment. Plus, I wanted my staff women to feel special and valued. I had *never*. In my *life*. Stayed at such a swanky place. So in preparation for the trip, I researched how much to tip for valet parking, concierge services, housekeeping, etc.

Side note: I am a HUGE believer in generous tipping. I tip at budget hotels. I start at 20% for food servers in restaurants, regardless of the service. I just think that my God is a generous God, and I want to reflect that to my world. Plus, why on earth wouldn't I want to brighten some hardworking housekeeper's day? I mean, picture this: you have to clean hotel rooms all day. Hotel rooms! People trash hotel rooms. They do gross things in hotel rooms because they know they won't have to clean it up! And you spend every day doing just that. So you walk into my room, and there's $5 laying on the bed *and* a fridge stocked with all the food and drinks we thought we'd eat and drink during our stay (but never do). BOOM! I like doing that for people.

Incidentally, during my research I found out that I am an over-tipper, even by Ritz standards. That's good. I was just desperately afraid of being an under-tipper or an awkward-tipper. Ever watch the *Seinfeld* episode where Elaine, George, and Jerry take turns trying to tip the host into getting them a table at the Chinese restaurant? Watch it. That's my fear. I want to be generous, but am afraid of looking weird doing it. Anyway, I did my research but was still worried that I'd look like the country bumpkin I am (or was) walking into the Ritz. Now, you're far enough into this book to know that *what-will-people-think-of-me* thoughts are TOTALLY against my philosophy of life. But they were kicking around in my head, just a little bit.

Back to our trip. So there it was, the huge lobby of the Ritz-Carlton, with rich old people sitting in huge wingbacks at mahogany tables, sipping ancient Scotch, dripping diamonds, and discussing in genteel Southern accents the travesty of the current presidential administration... and here come Tracy, Britney, and Diane and me, happily traipsing through, pulling our squeaky rolling suitcases. Well, they would have been squeakier if that gas station guy hadn't taken pity on us and brought over his can of WD-40 to rescue us. (We have a picture of him to prove that chivalry still exists in the South.)

We came in the backside of the building. This meant parading through the entire lobby before reaching the front desk. And now kicks in Kelly's social-skill-survival instinct. I see a photographer setting up for a shoot, and say, "Ya working?"

"Yep," he says.

"Is it a wedding?" I ask.

"It is."

"Do you love your job?" I ask.

"I do." And then we proceed to talk for a couple of minutes about what he does and why he enjoys it. I then continue my walk through intimidation-land to meet the remarkably clean, navy-blue-suited staff at the front desk.

Why did I stop and talk to the guy? I'm sure my girlfriends wondered too. (Actually, they know my mom—who's never met a stranger—so I'm sure they don't wonder all that much.) I thought through this later and realized that when I am feeling uneasy about how I fit in a situation, the best thing to do is shift my focus from *me* to *someone else*. The cool part? Almost everyone enjoys talking about themselves. And if I'm asking the questions and getting to know them, I don't have the capacity to think about how they're judging me! And they don't have time to judge me, because they're talking! And when I walk away, I hope they have a lingering impression that feels something like the love of Jesus.

I did this again with the concierge as we checked our bags to be held until our room was ready. "Do you love your job?"

"I do."

"Is it hard sometimes, dealing with crabby people?"

Her response surprised and delighted me: "I am empowered to do whatever it takes to solve a guest's problem." Well, that launched a conversation about organizations empowering front-line employees to take care of customers without needing a supervisor or approval from someone higher-up. The concierge and I had this understanding in common, and once again, I navigated an unfamiliar situation by drawing another person into a conversation where she felt respected and valued. And in the process, *I set myself at ease.*

You may be thinking, "So, Kelly, you befriended the hotel staff and a photographer. Maybe you blessed *them* and became comfortable with *them,* but what about the fancy-schmancy people who looked like they *lived* there? How did you get past feeling judged or worrying

about what they thought as they looked down their noses at you? "
(And a couple did, I'll tell you. But that's mostly because I was sitting
on the floor of the bathroom lounge. So classy.)

Well, here's the other side of this. This is the philosophy that keeps me
from being intimidated by people the world thinks are special, like
wealthy people, celebrities, and people of influence:

I'm a daughter of the King. My Father the King granted me a luxurious
stay in a beautiful place. I had every right to be there. There's royalty
in my blood, and this gives me the strength and courage to look with
love on every person my eyes meet, whether it's a parking valet or the
King of Sweden.

I have permission – no, I have a *responsibility* – to represent the love
and grace of my Father. I am to be intimidated by NO ONE's external
image. Externals deceive. The wealthy woman with the frou-frou
puppy in her purse struggles with the same insecurities as the
housekeeper. And both of them are equally loved by Jesus, just like
me. He gave His life for both the photographer and the occupant of
the penthouse suite. My job as His daughter is to share His love with
both. If that's my role, I have no business being intimidated by anyone.

The moral of this story? Well, a couple of things, I guess.

A) The Ritz-Carlton is awesome. Their staff is delightful, and I am
forever ruined, because no other hotel will compare.

B) Being confident to twirl in an intimidating setting comes first of all
by getting over yourself and seeking to encourage someone else.
You're a princess! You have royal blood! You are confident and relaxed
in any situation, because the people around you just need to feel the
love of Jesus coming from you. It's your job to make others feel
accepted; it's not their job to reach out to you.

This is a scriptural concept, you know? The Bible tells us, *Be humble,
thinking of others as better than yourselves. Don't look out only for*

your own interests, but take an interest in others, too. Philippians 2:3-4

Here's the thing. If you go into a situation judging others by their position or state in life, you'll automatically gauge where you are in the social scale and behave accordingly. For example, as I walked into the Ritz, I could assume that the wealthy guests are "better" than me, and that the bellhop would be "less than" me. I would then treat the bellhop as less valuable, and try to impress/please the wealthy person. How stressful is that?! I would be trying to look out for my own interests. My own interests would include wanting to be liked and included, to look like I belonged. So I could pretend I'm someone I'm not or brag about who I am or my life. I could talk about me-me-me and hope to impress.

Instead, if I go with the Bible's guide, I'll simply assume that everyone is worthy of being treated well, and I will look after *their* interests instead of *mine.* What's everyone interested in? Having their day brightened. Being approved of. Being respected. Hearing a compliment. A smile. A listening ear. Sometimes, a prayer.

Proactively blessing someone else strikes down the fear that no one will bless you. And, true to the law of planting and reaping, God will make sure you're taken care of, too.

Hey, guess what. This philosophy can guide all interactions as you twirl through your day. Walking into a store to make a return, assuming the cashier will be against you – or feeling defensive about getting "your way" – is looking out only for your own interests. And it sure doesn't make you any friends or speed the process of getting you what you need! (People are WAY more likely to go out of their way to help a friendly person than a demanding one.) Going in with the goal of encouraging the cashier while you do your business is honoring to Jesus and sets you on the path to receiving His blessings as you're living out your purpose as His daughter!

Philippians 2:14-16 says, *Go out into the world uncorrupted, a breath of fresh air in this squalid and polluted society. Provide people with a glimpse of good living and of the living God. Carry the light-giving Message into the night... (MSG)*

When you leave a social or business interaction, would the person say, "Wow! That chick's a breath of fresh air!" or would they be more likely to say, "Wow! I'm really glad she's gone." We never intend to be a downer, but it sometimes happens naturally because of our own worries or insecurities. However, when we exercise our looking-after-the-interests-of-others muscles, we'll become good at bringing fresh air instead.

I want to challenge you today to see every single interaction, from getting an oil change to a high school reunion to your daughter's dance recital, as an opportunity to exercise your royal duties of looking after the interests of others instead of your own.

Watch how God meets your needs as well, and you become more and more comfortable to twirl in your corner of the world.

74

Worth it All

───────◆───────

It was an overcast day as we stood at Aunt Julaine's gravesite. She was my Grandma Coulter's sister. Their two brothers, Uncles Roger and Rolly (short for Roland), stood there as well, with Grandpa, Julaine's kids (and my childhood playmates) Phillip, Kyla and Timothy, plus various spouses, children, friends, and me.

I suppose the minister said a few words, and probably read Psalm 23. We were sad but not despairing. We know where Aunt Julaine went, and we were glad she was done fighting the cancer. She had spent years as a missionary in Papua New Guinea, and many more years being Jesus to the people around her in Wisconsin, doing nice things like recommending and shipping essential oils to people like me who lived in other places but still benefited from her wisdom about natural treatments and remedies.

It was a quiet moment after it seemed all the words had been said, and then little old Uncle Rolly's voice rose up in spontaneous song from deep in his heart.

IT WILL BE WORTH IT ALL—

We immediately all caught on to the old hymn and joined in.

When we see Jesus.

Our sorrows seem so small

When we see Christ.

One glimpse of His dear face

All sorrows will erase.

So bravely run the race

'Til we see Christ![1]

The mix of voices, young and old, rose to Heaven, where Aunt Julaine was surely looking on, having changed from a nurturer on earth to a witness in Heaven as the rest of us continue to run our race.

Therefore, since we are surrounded by such a huge crowd of witnesses to the life of faith, let us strip off every weight that slows us down, especially the sin that so easily trips us up. And let us run with endurance the race God has set before us. Hebrews 12:1

For our present troubles are small and won't last very long. Yet they produce for us a glory that vastly outweighs them and will last forever! 2 Corinthians 4:17

Dear friends, know that in this world you will have struggles. You can give up and hunker down with your Doritos and Moose Tracks ice cream, or you can choose an eternal perspective. Hear the voices of those who have gone before you, calling out the greatness God placed in you.

Do not despair.

Do not give up.

The sorrow will not last forever.

Beyond the pain is the payoff. Maybe not in this lifetime, but this is the short one.

Eternity in the presence of Christ, that's what's real.

Bravely run your race.

It will be worth it all when you walk into eternity and see those you helped to lead there.

It will be worth it all when you see Jesus.

75

A LOVELY WAY TO LIVE

———————◆———————

1. Believe that you are favored.

> *Even before he made the world, God loved us and chose us in Christ to be holy and without fault in his eyes. God decided in advance to adopt us into his own family by bringing us to himself through Jesus Christ. This is what he wanted to do, and it gave him great pleasure. Ephesians 1:4-5*

Before God made the oceans and mountains and stars, He thought of you. He planned to bring you into His royal family.

Through Jesus, you can start fresh today. Simply accept His forgiveness for your sins—your regrets and failures that separate you from a holy God—and ask Him to lead your life!

2. Know that God is inviting you to become part of the greatest story in human history.

For we are God's masterpiece. He has created us anew in Christ Jesus, _so we can do_ the good things he planned for us long ago. _Ephesians 2:10_

God does not do a transforming work in your life so you can _lounge_. He does it so you can _live_. So that you can live out the true destiny that He has planned for you. This is HIS plan that He is inviting you to step into. Imagine how you will thrive if you do what you were uniquely designed by your Creator to do!

3. Shout down the doubts by believing that God's power will do it through you – and nothing is impossible with God.

> _I also pray that you will understand the incredible greatness of God's power for us who believe him. This is the same mighty power that raised Christ from the dead and seated him in the place of honor at God's right hand in the heavenly realms. Ephesians 1:19-20_

In our world, ultimate power is the ability to cheat death.

Jesus is like, "Been there, done that. And, by the way, that same energy flows in you."

God's resurrection power raised Jesus after He was three-days dead.

God's resurrection power gives you new life, when you choose to believe and follow Him.

God's resurrection power continues to be available to you every single day for the rest of your life.

If you've ever felt inadequate or weak as a follower of Jesus, this promise should fix you right up.

It says if you believe and live in His truth, the resurrection power of Jesus is yours! Your job is to simply believe and roll with it!

4. Throw open your arms and say, "Whatever."

Just say, whatever it is, God, I'm willing to let You do Your thing in my life.

I'll listen.

I'll learn.

I'll obey.

I'll have the hard conversations and risk being criticized and rejected by people who don't understand.

I'll stop indulging in my safe, anonymous life where no one knows who I am, but no one can hurt me.

I'll throw open my arms and let You twirl me.

"For I know the plans I have for you," says the Lord. "They are plans for good and not for disaster, to give you a future and a hope." Jeremiah 29:11

And your life will be blessed.

"Blessed" in Scripture literally means "happy".

You are blessed [happy] because you believed that the Lord would do what he said. Luke 1:45

God has a good plan for you. As His daughter, His power is in you.

Walk into your destiny. Be blessed. Be happy.

Throw your arms wide and twirl.

About the Author

———————◆———————

Kelly Dykstra used to think she was just along for the ride in life, but then God and her super-hot husband empowered her to stand on her own two feet (usually in sweet high heels) and go after her own destiny. She's passionate about freeing other women up to do the same.

Kelly uses writing and speaking to simplify Biblical truth and shed fresh light on the faith journey. Her sense of humor and dynamic teaching style connect with a wide variety of audiences, both men and women.

Her favorite things (in no particular order) include Heinz Genuine Dill Pickles, thinking about home decorating, massages, traveling, and finding Happy Hour specials in St. Paul, Minnesota, with Eric and their kiddos, Aidan (14), Holland (16), and Braden (20).

You can find Kelly on Instagram (@KellyDykstra) and on Facebook (PastorKellyDykstra).

Eric and Kelly co-founded The Crossing, a multi-site church near Minneapolis, MN, in 2004. You can find The Crossing, videos of Eric and Kelly's messages, and stream worship services live at freegrace.tv.

You can also find information about (and watch) Twirl, Kelly's annual event for women, at freegrace.tv/more/twirl.

The People Mover

By Kelly Dykstra

God has seen your future. It is good. He's come back to take you there. God is not in Heaven biting His nails, wondering if you'll make the right choices and guessing how it's all going to turn out for you. He's calmly waiting for you to relax and let Him carry you forward in life.

The question is: will you ditch a stressed-out faith in your own effort and step into a remarkably effortless journey with the Designer of your destiny?

With candor, humor, and just a drop of sarcasm, Kelly is a friend who will tell it like it is. She provides a practical, inspiring guide for making the switch to step on The People Mover. Your faith journey will never look the same.

Available on Amazon and Amazon Kindle.

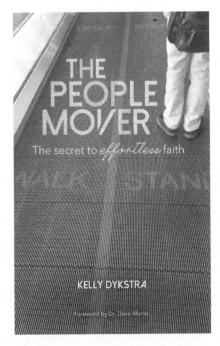